To Joe and Olga —

Thank you for your many
kindnesses and for your
instruction about American
politics and our military —

Best regards —

The Trump Phenomenon and The Future of US Foreign Policy

The Trump Phenomenon and The Future of US Foreign Policy

Daniel Quinn Mills
Harvard Business School, USA

Steven Rosefielde
University of North Carolina at Chapel Hill, USA

World Scientific

NEW JERSEY · LONDON · SINGAPORE · BEIJING · SHANGHAI · HONG KONG · TAIPEI · CHENNAI · TOKYO

Published by

World Scientific Publishing Co. Pte. Ltd.

5 Toh Tuck Link, Singapore 596224

USA office: 27 Warren Street, Suite 401-402, Hackensack, NJ 07601

UK office: 57 Shelton Street, Covent Garden, London WC2H 9HE

Library of Congress Cataloging-in-Publication Data
Names: Mills, Daniel Quinn, author. | Rosefielde, Steven, author.
Title: The Trump phenomenon and the future of US foreign policy / by Daniel Quinn Mills,
    Harvard Business School, USA, and Steven Rosefielde, University of North Carolina, USA.
Description: Hackensack, NJ : World Scientific Publishing Co. Pte. Ltd., 2016.
Identifiers: LCCN 2016036154| ISBN 9789813200876 | ISBN 9789813200999 (pbk)
Subjects: LCSH: United States--Foreign relations--21st century. | Trump, Donald, 1946---Influence.
Classification: LCC E895 .M55 2016 | DDC 327.73009/051--dc23
LC record available at https://lccn.loc.gov/2016036154

British Library Cataloguing-in-Publication Data
A catalogue record for this book is available from the British Library.

Desk Editors: Dong Lixi/Edward C. Yong
Typeset by Stallion Press

Email: enquiries@stallionpress.com

Printed in Singapore by B & Jo Enterprise Pte Ltd

Executive Summary

American foreign policy in recent decades has not benefitted the American people. It has cost them many good jobs, cut their real incomes, raised their taxes, cut benefits, and imperiled their lives. Since World War II, American foreign policy has been cosmopolitan in nature at the expense of the common man. It has enriched insiders while harming the American middle and working classes. Donald Trump's popularity is a reflection of these discontents. This book explains these popular frustrations and proposes a sane policy for America that benefits its people generally, without attributing the policy to Trump. Trump has touched America's raw nerve, and the problems he senses are real. The problems can be rectified regardless of the adequacy of his prescriptions. He is leading a crusade. In this book we are illuminating what can be realistically accomplished.

The principles and many details of an alternative policy based on democratic nationalism are described in this book. Democratic nationalism presumes that America is a large family in which the needs of members of the family should not be sacrificed to those of people abroad or to the interests of establishment insiders in the US.

American foreign policy should have six basic characteristics which our current policy, formed from a mélange of approaches benefitting private interests, does not have. American policy should be:

- Complete,
- Comprehensive,

- Coherent,
- Consistent,
- Credible, and
- Compliant.

The underlying principles of American policy should be:

1. Build foreign policy strictly on the principle of core national interest — not insider interest and domestic politics.
2. Work for these objectives on a consensus building basis domestically and diplomatically in international affairs — we should not coerce ordinary people into accepting a special interest driven "new normal" and we should resort to force only when it is made necessary by defense against armed aggression.
3. Oppose only one major adversary at a time in foreign affairs, not all potential adversaries at once as we are doing now, unless compelled by events to do so. Prioritize foreign challenges and allocate resources accordingly.
4. Restore America's founding constitutional principles, and promote beneficial government abroad, not simply our own rancorous form of democracy.
5. Quit appearing on the domestic and international stages as if we were no more than platitude-spouting hypocrites.
6. Assert the interests of ordinary Americans at home and our national interests in preference to those of other nations.
7. Conduct domestic programs efficiently and any foreign interventions well, including having an exit strategy.
8. Keep our eyes on the major things and do not get distracted.
9. Never lose sight of our most promising opportunity and of our most dangerous potential adversary.
10. Be clear about our objectives, not muddle-headed.
11. Do not compartmentalize too much.
12. Be prepared to pay the economic and social cost for power.

Specifically, on the foreign policy front the United States should:

1. Accept that we have reentered a multipolar world, and cease trying to impose American hegemony through globalization, liberalization, unrestricted migration, faux democratization, and the rule of Western law;
2. Build a foreign policy that maximizes the domestic welfare of ordinary Americans instead of quixotic and easily abused idealistic agendas to create heaven on earth;
3. Seek a Cold Peace with Russia, rather than the second Cold War which is now being decried by many observers;
4. Contain Iranian ambitions in order to weaken a rival and preserve our access to a critical region of the globe;
5. Accept a restructuring of national borders in the Middle East;
6. Contain China — in order to restrain a rival and preserve our access to another critical region of the globe;
7. Strengthen Japan — in order to help restrain China;
8. Strengthen India — in order to help restrain China;
9. Permit the European Union to evolve in whatever direction works out — even if it falls apart;
10. Alter our trade policies to seek to maintain and reestablish high-wage goods-producing companies.

Sane policy is very different from what is now being practiced by the American government. To see this, it is necessary to realize that a policy should be judged by its results, not by its publicly stated intentions. The results of present policies are violent chaos in and around the Muslim world and the increasing hostility of our Russian and Chinese rivals. Thus, the evidence is that prevailing policies are misguided and inept.

The current Administration has a perspective: anti-colonialism. Trump's perspective is very different: democratic nationalism.

The current Administration has an international orientation which involves subordination of the United States to international norms and organizations. Trump's orientation is very different: American strategic independence.

The current Administration has no preparation for crafting a strategy and confuses tactics with strategy. Sane policy begins with a clear strategic concept, as is described in this book.

The Obama Administration uses the term "strategic patience" to camouflage its indecision and inaction. Critics coined the phrase, "leading from behind," to characterize its inability to provide direction to the world. Sane policy is characterized by decision and action; it is able to give direction to the world about American desires and intentions.

While Donald Trump has raised the level of discussion of these ideas in American public life, he does not have a monopoly on them. The shifts in American foreign policy which are envisioned in this book can be made by any president and any political party. The shifts and the considerations which motivate them are deserving of careful attention by any American chief executive. This is neither a Republican agenda, nor a Democratic one. We believe that it is an American agenda.

Contents

Foreword

This book addresses a momentous topic. It asks if the United States can alter its foreign policy even though it has been on the same course since World War II. The book rests on the belief that the elites which control both major political parties in America can be persuaded to alter a course that has benefitted them greatly while failing to benefit the American people as a whole. Or, if that cannot be done, then perhaps the elites can be weakened to the extent that they can no longer successfully defend their international advantages. We view our role as authors to be Socrates-like gadflies of today's American electorate. Our book concerns what might happen if a new President were to achieve sufficient reform of the political and economic systems of the United States that a policy much more in the interest of the American middle and working classes could be pursued. Such a policy would be sane in the perceptions of the American people, rather than the insider-benefitting policy we have been following and which seems insane to them. American policy in recent presidencies seems to our people insane because it does not benefit them, even though they are told that it does. So why is our government doing it? Isn't there some alternative that is sane?

There is a serious need for reform. Things can go very badly in human affairs. For example, the Great Depression was foreseen and could have been avoided. World War II was foreseen and could have been avoided. Neither was avoided. But our nation survived the

Depression and the war that followed. In retrospect, our nation regrets our failure to avoid the Great Depression and we romanticize the fighting of the Second World War, pretending that it was inevitable. The war was not at all inevitable and it would have been better to avoid both the Depression and the war.

The world is now on a course that makes likely both new economic and military catastrophes. They can be foreseen. Both are now being widely predicted. Because they are foreseen, they can be avoided, and that would be a very good thing.

It is with the hope that our country can change course and avoid future disasters that we offer this book.

Preface

Many Americans have been surprised by important events in recent years. The Financial Crisis was a surprise for some (the American government insists it was a surprise for all, but this is disingenuous — one of the authors of this book predicted a major financial crisis with correct timing in a book following the dot. com crisis of a few years before). Other surprises have included the rise of ISIS, the continuing near-stagnation of earnings in the American economy, and the nomination of Donald Trump as the candidate of the Republican Party for the American presidency in the election of 2016. Where there are repeated surprises, the way a person thinks about world events must be ineffective. His or her filter for separating noise from signal must be defective.

People often think that they simply need more information and they will be better able to anticipate the future. They go to the news media and experts and conferences. But since their filters are defective, they cannot tell what is important and what is not, and they are continually surprised by events. The problem is more than lack of enough information.

Only with an effective framework for interpreting information can a person recognize what is a preferable national policy. Our purpose is to provide that framework and to provide examples of its useful application.

Part I

A Successful American Foreign Policy

Americans should be less concerned about what we have been doing or not doing; even about the difficulties in which we currently find ourselves. We should be most concerned about where we are headed — about where we should be going. This is the topic of our next chapters.

Chapter 1

A Challenge To Us All

Donald Trump is a phenomenon. He has called for an about-face in American foreign policy. Many of his criticisms reflect the public mood, but he has not yet devised a carefully-considered alternative because his barbs are often contradictory. This is his challenge. Diagnosing the disease is not enough. He has to go further by designing an optimal therapy.

Trump's opponents have challenged him to prove that he can offer a better alternative to the postwar American establishment consensus, implying that he is talking out of his hat; that there are no superior options.

This book suggests that Trump's intuition is often correct, even though he has not devised a cogent therapy yet. We do not pretend to speak for Trump, but show that a sane American foreign policy that adjusts America's postwar trajectory can be accomplished if our leaders have the courage and integrity to do so.

The shifts in American foreign policy which are envisioned in this book can be made by any president and any political party. The shifts and the considerations which motivate them are deserving of careful attention by any American chief executive. This is not a Republican agenda, nor a Democratic one. We believe that it is an American agenda.

The United States has been on the same policy course for seventy years. The course is now being challenged more strongly than ever before. Because the internationalist cosmopolitan policy course has benefitted primarily insiders and has harmed our segments of our society, it seems wrongheaded to many. Therefore, there are many discussions of the course and its limitations. Its defenders demand that its critics offer a complete and coherent alternative. This book is an effort to see if that can be done. Of what would an alternative — a sane policy consist? Can one be fashioned that is complete and coherent and is potentially a viable alternative to the course on which we have been traveling?

We are examining an alternative to the internationalist cosmopolitan position which the United States has assumed over the past seventy years. To contrast an alternative to the current American policy orientation we label Trump's alternative democratic nationalism. Democratic nationalism presumes that America is a large family in which the needs of members of the family should not be sacrificed to those of people abroad or to the interests of establishment insiders in the US. We do not mean by "national" something that is "retro-national" — like American isolationism or European fascism.

"Nationalist" and "cosmopolitan" are not precise designations, but are clearer than those which are now being used in the political process in our country.

The political process currently speaks of internationalist and nationalist positions when it stoops from vitriol to dealing with this extraordinarily important matter. The problem is not with the term "nationalist," however loosely it may be defined, but with the term "internationalist." This is because any foreign policy is necessarily internationalist, and to ignore this is to risk a pernicious misunderstanding.

Modern American internationalism is best described as a form of cosmopolitanism in which the decision-making of a nation (often referred to as its national sovereignty) is subordinated via treaties or organizational memberships to multi-national bodies in the belief that abiding by outsiders' interests, America best promotes its own wellbeing. Cosmopolitanism holds, roughly, that the United States should act in the world primarily as part of coalitions of nations such as the United Nations and our various military alliances. It holds also that the United States should shoulder a major portion of the burden of assisting other countries in common defense and in human improvement undertakings. It holds that the United States should support the economic development of other nations primarily through trade agreements which promote globalization of our economy and foreign economic assistance. Finally, modern cosmopolitanism holds that the United States should sponsor in other countries democracy, human rights initiatives, environmental initiatives and other forms of social advocacy. Ostensibly to support these various purposes, the United States supports international initiatives. To support the American system of military alliances, the United States supports the military and domestic activities of many foreign governments. All this creates what is perceived by many Americans to be a form of give-away cosmopolitanism.

The problem with contemporary cosmopolitan internationalist policy is not that it aspires to encompass everything, but that it is dogmatic for the benefit of insiders. Both major American political parties largely support modern cosmopolitanism, though they argue about its specific provisions.

When challenged, cosmopolitanism is most vigorously defended on the basis of the alleged shortcomings of anti-cosmopolitan postures in our past; in particular, the isolationism of the 1930s and the nativism of the early twentieth century. Isolationism is said to have led to World War II and nativism to discrimination against minorities. It is not our purpose to explore these indictments, but later chapters will show that today's nationalist perspective is quite different from that of isolationists or nativists of the past.

Many Americans today offer a strong indictment of the cosmopolitanism that has dominated our policy since World War II. The indictment is that internationalist cosmopolitanism (including feckless military adventurism) has bankrupted the country (America's official national debt is now almost twenty trillion dollars, and its unofficial debt is much more), has impoverished the working and middle classes through the loss of manufacturing and related jobs, and has failed to protect our national security against the rise of strong antagonists in China, Russia and militant Islam.

The critics of cosmopolitanism have been ridiculed and ignored for several decades. In recent months, however, they have gathered enough strength to challenge cosmopolitanism strongly and to nominate a presidential candidate. In this book, we wish to examine the policy alternative they now represent.

The Debate Over Nationalism And Cosmopolitanism

We are discussing nationalism and cosmopolitanism in a context of internationalism. We and our readers must be careful because every term is politically loaded. We use "national" to mean a unit for effective democratic governance which also is sensitive to core cultural traditions. Nationalism as we conceive it is inclusive and democratic. It is contrasted with cosmopolitanism which is basically elitist and insider-dominated. The basic issue is who rules the country — an establishment or its people?

Trump proposes what might be considered a government policy that preserves core American political culture, including our Constitution, and serves ordinary Americans. This may involve both domestic and international policy.

We use the term "cosmopolitan" to mean an attitude that wants to rule globally and obliterate western core culture in favor of approved forms of multiculturalism (some cultures are arbitrarily deemed deserving; others tainted). Cosmopolitans aren't over-committed although they seek to put a finger in everything, because they aren't committed to their rhetorical commitments. They will not fight major powers on their turf or the periphery. Their only commitment is to using the national treasury to advance insiders' tactical objectives.

We recognize the danger in using a dichotomy like democratic nationalism and cosmopolitanism to discuss what are actually multi-faceted differences in opinion which have many nuances and even contradictions. For example, on what is called the "right," there is an important distinction between liberal (in the Enlightenment usage) and conservative (in the modern usage). On the "left", there is Marxism and there is Social Democratic "liberalism" with a long history of bitter antagonism between them. Yet, political commentators often refer to "right" and "left" when there is no simple dichotomy.

The political debate is controlled by false dichotomies that many smart people accept rather than clarify. There are in fact a multitude of false dichotomies in today's political debate. In America we seem to prefer things in twos. We have two major political parties and we make dichotomous distinctions between them. The Republicans are for this; the Democrats are for that. It keeps things simple for an electorate that is continually distracted.

This book takes a position in the forefront of the debate between national and cosmopolitan attitudes, which is an intellectual but not academic debate. We address the political intellectual debate which is carried on in such venues as the publications of the American Enterprise Institute, the Brookings Institution, the Hoover Institution, the Carnegie Institution, *the New York Times*, *the Washington Post*, *the New Yorker*, *the Wall Street Journal*, *the New York Review of Books*, *the Claremont Review of Books* and *Foreign Affairs*. In the political intellectual debate terms are much less well-defined than in the academic debate and much that is important is very fuzzy. In other publications, including *Blind Faith* which is soon to be released, we address primarily the academic inquiry into these matters.

The political intellectual debate is well-phrased now in terms of nationalism and cosmopolitanism. Recently, Dalibor Rohac, writing in a publication of the American Enterprise Institute (AEI) asked, "Who will stand up for cosmopolitanism?" Rohac observed that "There seems to be an emerging consensus on the center-right that an excess of cosmopolitanism is at least partly to blame for the wave of populism that is sweeping across politics on both sides of the Atlantic." He then quoted Ross Douthat at *The New York Times* who argued that a cosmopolitan worldview just a "powerful caste's self-serving explanation for why it alone deserves to rule the world." In contrast, Rohac cites his colleague at AEI, Tim Carney, as seeing the British vote to leave the European Union as a victory of nationalist tribalism over an equally closed-minded cosmopolitan version.

Rohac also observes that this controversy is not brand new. "At a meeting of the free-market Mont Pèlerin Society two years ago, one of its senior members complained bitterly about 'cosmopolitan, selfish individuals 'floating' at the surface and searching for short-term pleasures and advantages — without roots and responsibility' and suggested that the world needed instead 'responsible citizens anchored in domestic realities.'"

Rohac then states his own position on the controversy. "I beg to differ," he writes. "the problem is not an excess of cosmopolitanism but rather its absence, especially on the conservative, free-market right. Lionel Robbins, who was at the foundation of the Mont Pèlerin Society — the intellectual home of the free-enterprise movement — called nationalism "the nauseating backwash of historical mysticism and geographical particularism which is threatening to destroy our common culture."

There is merit to Rohac's observations. It is important not to go too far in the direction of the new nationalism we are suggesting here. It is important to be able to return to liberal (in the classic sense) economic globalization when it becomes possible. The problem, of course, is that the liberal global prescription has been in recent decades only theoretical — that it has not been real; that trade agreements have been anything but open, free trade.

Also, if nationalism means, as it does to many European intellectuals, fascism, then it should not be supported. Nationalism does not mean fascism in America. We do not have a fascist past. We have a past which involves racism and exploitation of an industrial working class. But we do not have a history of fascist militarism such as occurred in Italy, Germany, Japan and other countries. To deny this is to ignore the twelve-year duel between Hitler in Germany and Franklin D. Roosevelt in the United States which ended in Hitler's suicide and the destruction of fascism virtually worldwide.

America does have a past which is full of leftist claims that there is an American fascism, but that is not reality, it is political myth. Still, if nationalism and fascism have been made synonymous in the public and intellectual mind, then another term will have to be coined for the sort of own-family orientation which we mean by the term democratic nationalism.

Uncertain Americans

Americans are uncertain about Trump's impact on America's role in the world. Uncertainty is more prominent than in the past because our policy — specifically in response to challenges from terrorists, Russia and China — is playing a major role in Trump's presidential campaign.

Despite the growing criticism of cosmopolitanism, some Americans remain strongly supportive of it.

One of the authors recently heard a speech given by one of the most important investors in the United States. He runs a multi-billion dollar public employee retirement system. Briefly, he stated that since the collapse of the USSR, we are living in the age of the American Empire. He added that "empires last for hundreds of years," and concluded that we and our children will all live in a very favorable period economically and in terms of national security. His is a perspective that supports cosmopolitanism and its consequences.

Other Americans are less supportive. A much-broadcast political commentator recently said that he was most worried about the degree of disorder unfolding globally. He shared an acronym that West Point faculty members use to describe the world their students are inheriting: VUCA — volatile, uncertain, chaotic, ambivalent.

It is a strong criticism of cosmopolitanism that it has brought our country to a very high level of danger of a major conflict in the last year of the Obama Administration. The danger is a consequence of the combination of

1. A cunning Russian leader who may over-reach; with
2. A Chinese military which is increasingly assertive and may not be under effective civilian control (which would mirror the circumstance in Japan which permitted the beginning of World War II in Asia); and
3. An Iranian leadership which is an implacable enemy of the United States and is steadily increasing its reach and strength; and
4. An American President given to confused signals and indecision.

What Does It Mean To Be An American Democratic Nationalist?

To be an American democratic nationalist means to be concerned about our fellow country-persons and to care what happens to them. It means not to throw their livelihoods aside in favor of privileged people in other countries without seeing that our citizens get something else which is valuable. It means not to put them at risk physically from terrorists or criminals when risk can be prevented. It means not to watch them drift into sloughs of despair and drugs without trying to help them. It means to see that the system is not rigged against them. It means not to join the elitists who are cosmopolitan and despise many or most of our fellow citizens.

A Special Role For The United States

Cosmopolitanism asserts a special role for the United States in the world. It is a leadership role (whether imagined to be exercised from front or rear). In general, America has a special role in the world because it is perhaps the least hated of the great nations, an accident of its recent birth. But a special role does not mean that America is responsible for all other nations and peoples. A special role need not convey to Americans an affirmative mission to direct the political and economic evolution of humanity. Instead, it may be that the most important thing America can do in the world is return to a nationalist perspective which is better understood by other nations than is a generally charitable posture, one easily interpreted abroad as hypocritical.

Keeping America Safe

Underneath the changing attitudes of Americans toward our role in the world lies the apparent failure of several of our major military interventions since World War II. In addition is the evident rise of the military strength and international assertiveness of other major powers. We no longer win every conflict and we no longer are the singularly dominant power. Even ardent cosmopolitans such as Hillary Clinton accept that

America must adjust to limitations on its power and to the new correlation of power in the world.

In fact, it appears that the seven pillars of modern American cosmopolitanism are each crumbling:

- Economic globalism is giving way to competitive currency devaluations.
- The Western world order championed by the United States is being rejected by major powers including Russia, China and Iran.
- The collective security upon which America relies seems increasingly unable to achieve success (in the Middle East and Ukraine, for example).
- American hegemony in what appeared a unipolar world is giving way to a world of multiple great powers.
- American interventionism seems less and less effective (as for example, in Syria, Iraq, Libya, Afghanistan, Ukraine and Cuba) — it seems often undertaken for the wrong reasons and without methods of exit in mind.
- Cosmopolitanism which the United States has long sponsored, especially with respect to the European Union, seems increasingly fragile.
- International governance which also the United States has long sponsored, especially via the United Nations and its affiliated agencies, seems also increasingly ineffective in the world.

Cosmopolitanism As Practiced By The Obama Administration

The most recent demonstrations of America's cosmopolitanism have been provided by the Obama Administration. There are many, many examples. Here we take only one which seems to us particularly instructive.

On December 1, 2015, Stephen Crowley of the New York Times published a photo taken in Paris at the climate summit of the silver-haired and immaculately-dressed American Secretary of State, John Kerry, towering over a smaller, indifferently-attired Vladimir Putin and waving a finger in Putin's face. Putin stared at Kerry with bitter expression and angry eyes.

The photo is an apt expression of current American policy — a distant and arrogant President and a bullying Secretary of State attempting to dictate to the world a new world order — a peculiar mixture of idealistic posturing and personal self-interest in which the national interest of the United States plays little role. In particular, the United States government has announced several times in recent years that the world has outgrown and abandoned realpolitik — the contest of nations for international advantage.

We do not endorse realpolitik. But we are realists and we recognize that it still plays a significant role in international politics. It is a game many nations continue to play. It is not for the West to decide unilaterally that the world has abandoned realpolitik. Putin has decided to reinvigorate it; China and Iran are doing the same. The West pretends realpolitik is ended; it is not. The Obama Administration's policy appears as feckless in a world in which it insists a game being played by other key contestants is one in which the United States will not participate. We deny that international relations should be played by the rules of realpolitik — but we are not able to set the rules unilaterally. And the West's arrogance in pretending to set the rules becomes both an issue in international affairs and a weakness for the West in the realpolitik game

This particular American policy attitude has created substantial back-lash. It is common for America's rivals to presume that American policy is dominated by American national interest and camouflaged by moral pretense. Whether or not this was ever the case is not worth debating, for it is no longer remotely accurate and can be confined to the dustbin of historical disputes now outdated. Instead, American policy is driven this way and that by the winds of private avarice and special interest social activism, and is denied any coherent rhyme or reason. In the venal minds of the people who represent America in international relations the slightest hope of private gain outweighs every consideration of public advantage.

But covering all private interest is a screen of moralism which American statespersons rarely fail to invoke. American and indeed most Western politicians continually describe their political positions as moral ones. This is evidenced by Secretary Kerry's admonitions to President Putin shown in the photo mentioned above.

A Brief History Of Modern American Cosmopolitanism

In the aftermath of the collapse of the Soviet Union the West sought to reorder the world in its own idealized image. That effort consumed some twenty-five years and was led by three American presidents, two of whom were Democrats and one Republican. That effort has failed.

The West has not yet acknowledged the failure and the United States has not provided leadership as to what follows in the wake of failure.

The world order is now being dictated in Moscow, Beijing and Tehran. It is incomplete, inconsistent and fraught with danger of conflict. It most closely resembles what Western leaders have denounced as realpolitik — a regime of international affairs which recent Western leaders had jettisoned.

The result is that our country is now of a very different opinion than several decades ago. Two generations ago, Americans basked in the afterglow of victory in World War II and were certain that the United States should play a significant role internationally. By 2014 a poll taken by the Pew Research Centre/ World Bank and published in *The Economist* on October 3, 2015, shows that the proportion of Americans who agree that "the United States should mind its own business internationally" has risen from 20% in 1964 to 52% in 2014. To modern nationalists, minding one's own business does not preclude international involvement and self-defense. It only means that we should stop trying to impose our values on the world while actually serving insider special interests.

A Realist Perspective

Most modern nationalists appear to believe themselves to be realists — objective in their assessments and paying attention to the actions of other people, not to their words. Words are intentionally misleading.

Full realism is necessary in order to understand the world on its own terms. It is alright to have ideals and purposes, but they must not be allowed to undermine objectivity. Wishful thinking is the great sin — it undermines objectivity and makes realism impossible. In an idealist perspective, such as that of cosmopolitanism, realism becomes unacceptable and even distasteful. The Republicans insist that they are more realistic than the Democrats, and perhaps they are, but it is realism couched in the overall context of an idealistic cosmopolitanism. Wishful thinking has colored American policy-making for decades and has likely ended the short reign of America as the world's dominant power.

Many modern nationalists assess America's situation in the globe today as difficult and challenging but not dire; it is not grave. Our situation remains rather favorable, less because of what we have been doing than because of the difficulties in which our rivals find themselves. The Russians are emerging from a moderate economic recession driven by the low price of raw materials; the Chinese are grappling with an economic slowdown of uncertain origin; the Iranians are mired in foreign interventions in Iraq and Syria, and face increasing dissent at home. Despite these advantages to America, there are great dangers that we face, mainly because of own shortcomings. It is unreasonable to expect that our rivals will not surmount their current difficulties and increase the pressure they put on us. How well-prepared are we to meet increased pressure? Not well.

Cosmopolitan Over-Commitment

The Chinese are patient plotters; the Russians are opportunists; the Iranians are cautious zealots. The Chinese are not yet ready to challenge us; the Russians are forcefully challenging us in many arenas; the Iranians will challenge us in their own region. This situation calls for a sectoral response from America, always recognizing that what happens in one sector can be influenced from outside that sector.

In this context, it is no longer realistic to view the United States as the center of world politics. The pressure many nations face from Islamists; the pressure Southeast Asian nations face from China; and the pressure Eastern European nations face from Russia are all destabilizing. The United States is in fact peripheral to each of these situations. But the weaker party in each case will try to draw America into the conflicts on its side.

Modern cosmopolitans will always agree to be drawn in. This is because they are satisfied with the world status quo and see themselves as its defenders against anyone who should try to disrupt it. The result is a tendency for America to overcommit itself abroad.

Trying To Identify And Focus On The Key Issues

How close did we come to a major war when Turkey shot down a Russian fighter on November 24, 2015? The situation was reminiscent of the outbreak of World War I. Turkey is a member of NATO; if Turkey is attacked, the treaty requires the other NATO members to come to its aid. Yet, Turkey acted against the Russians without prior consultation with NATO. If Russia had retaliated strongly, a wider war might have begun before American and European leadership were even aware of the risk.

Russia appears to most Americans to be weak: its economy is in difficulty; its military is recovering from deep decay, yet it is seizing opportunities for aggression and intervention. How is this possible? In the longer term, will Russia be able to survive? If not, will it react increasingly violently to challenges to its sphere of influence? Is this what is happening now? How should the United States react to Russian assertiveness?

Trump proposes to destroy ISIS. Can ISIS be destroyed? If not, will it push more aggressively on its borders in Africa and Europe? It appears that Islamism is going to displace secularism and moderation (what the American media has identified as the color revolutions) in the Muslim world. But Islamism is split between Sunni and Shia. Will this split limit the success of Islamism? Should the United States ally with one against the other?

Will China accept frustration imposed by American power in the South China Sea? It has already used its Cambodian puppet state to stymie ASEAN's effort to contain Beijing in the South China Sea. If not, will it speed up its rearmament toward an early showdown?

Will Germany accept the European Union's dissolution as it presses to expand politically to the east? If not, will it use the threat of supra-national capital flight as a cudgel as it did against Greece in 2015 or turn to forms of force at some point to preserve the EU and/or the Euro Zone? The notion of Germany turning again to coercion is inconceivable to many European leaders and the elite who support them, but it should not be dismissed without careful concern. To dismiss the possibility would be just another example of wishful thinking.

Will the United States accept decreasing importance in each of these theaters? If not, will we become increasingly unpredictable and erratic in all our responses?

These are the key issues which American policy must face. Can today's nationalism provide intelligent answers to them?

Two Choices

Broadly, America faces two choices. Cosmopolitanism wishes to continue the regime of the past seventy years in which America sought to dominate the world first as the protector of freedom and after the collapse of the Soviet Union, as policeman of the world.

Modern American nationalism as represented by Donald Trump rejects this policy. It rejects hegemony as something for which the American electorate has little stomach and our government has no aptitude, and which is too expensive in lives and treasure.

Modern American nationalism also rejects full withdrawal (isolationism) as something for which the American electorate has little stomach and which is dangerous to our national security (because strong opponents can then arise abroad unchallenged by us). A more forward strategy is required.

We propose, therefore, general guidelines for America's international involvement.

War is always very unfortunate and should be avoided if possible. But it cannot always be avoided, nor should it be. President Abraham

Lincoln in his last war message to Congress on December 6, 1864, noted that between the rebels and the Union the unresolved issue was "distinct, simple, and inflexible. It is an issue which can only be tried by war, and decided by victory." Some things are of that nature and require armed conflict.

We should try to avoid situations in which the issue is distinct, simple and inflexible, because they justify war. Yet often our politicians, for their own benefit and that of their associates, so define international disagreements, and thus increase the risk of war.

In America today, policy is driven by private interests and is treated by those in power as a political management problem. All events are spun to protect the party in power. The result is failure when perceived from the position of the American middle and working classes. The major American commitment in policy as it is currently done does not work for the majority of the American people.

Chapter 2

The Best Path Toward National Security

Sane policy means replacing insiders in-command with public servants. It means preserving our core culture and re-directing government policy (domestic and foreign) to the public good.

Cosmopolitan policy is expressed in big government. But big government cannot fulfill its promises and only uses promises as a cover for inside maneuvering.

Sane policy rejects the claim of insiders that unless government does more, precious missions will remain unaccomplished.

Sanity means that America should not pretend to do the impossible as a cover for insider dealing.

Sound Policy

"…sound policy," observed Napoleon, "is nothing else than the calculation of combinations and chances…"

Calculation of combinations and chances is what the American government should have been doing these last few presidencies, and what it has failed to do. Instead, it has indulged itself in wishful thinking, personal interest and political posturing.

We have attempted in this book to make the sort of calculations of combinations and chances which the great Frenchman proposed. We have assessed the changing correlation of power among the major geo-political blocs, and determined what America's most likely successful policies will be.

By making calculations of combinations and chances, we develop sound policy. Trump's recommendations can be construed as a Jeffersonian-style policy (that is, pursuing national interest while attempting to remain at arm's-length with the controversies of the rest of the world) updated to incorporate the advantages of being a globally-engaged great power of the modern sort.

Our analysis shows that an effort to forge a more nationally-based policy can be attempted without any more danger than we are currently running with our policy of cosmopolitanism and with great prospect for success. We have drifted so far into cosmopolitanism that our country (though not its political and business elites) is suffering. The 2016 presidential campaign indicates that most Americans realize this.

Success for us is the pursuit of our lives in America in peace and freedom. But peace will not come easily. Its likelihood is now slipping away and must be regained.

Illusions About What Prevents War

People in the West are given to illusions in each era about what will prevent war. The notion always is that war is no longer likely because reason and interests prevent it.

In the later part of the nineteenth century people thought that high culture would prevent war. They pointed to Germany's literature, philosophy and opera; to Austria's music; to French literature and arts (decorative and fine); to Russia's literature and religious paintings; to Italy's operas; to Britain's literature. The notion was that as nations developed and shared high culture, bonds would be created which made war anachronistic. The First World War shattered that illusion and took high culture with it.

Another notion was that economic ties, in particular trade but also cross-border investments, would prevent wars. It was also shattered in the First World War.

After the First World War there emerged the notion that war had become so awful that it would not occur again — people of all nations would reject it because they had experienced its horror in the First

World War. Quite the contrary happened. Within 21 years after the end of the First World War another world war was underway.

In our era the notion that economic ties will obviate war has again emerged. People of different nations, it is insisted, have too much to lose economically to fight one another.

Why Technological Advance Does Not Guarantee Peace

As we have pointed out above, a major fallacy in American thinking is that worldwide economic ties and technological advances led by the United States will guarantee peace. Nations do not want to lose the advantages of international trade, it is affirmed. Also affirmed is that advances in communications technology (including the Internet and cellular phones) will promote democracy all over the world and will so raise human expectations that all nations will have to turn to Western-style consumerism to keep their populations pacified.

Both presumptions are wrong. Economic ties do push the world toward peace, but they are not determinative. Other factors play more important roles, including national aspirations, historical resentments, international rivalries and religious controversies.

Improvements in communications technology, like most technical advances, both support and undermine peace. Americans ordinarily greet technological advances with extravagant claims for their positive impact on the world. The Internet was supposed to bring democracy to China. It has not done so. It was supposed to combine with social media to bring Western-style modernization to the Islamic world. It has not done so. Instead, the Internet has brought tightened authoritarianism to China and to Russia; the Internet and the cell phone are used as weapons of cyber-conflict and as tools for terrorist recruiting.

Once in a while, technology far outruns human social development. Then there is a crash — not because of the technology, but in spite of it.

The castle technology is building, with all its wonderful apps, stands on sand. You say, "Technology has changed our lives," but it doesn't matter. Basic human drives, exhibited in political developments, are undermining all that technology promises.

Another social crash is coming. There will be political upheavals and warfare, and technology's promise will be lost.

Technology is now outrunning the ability of global politics to cope with the consequences of technological change. Historically, the consequence will be a major step backward for both economic globalism and technological progress.

The high culture advocates, the never-again generation, the economic ties crowd and the technology pundits correctly point to influences which weigh heavily against war. They just fail to give the devil his due by recognizing that the factors that drive toward war are powerful and often decisive.

The American attitude of cosmopolitan interventions abroad, as it has developed in the past five decades, is a major source of the conflicts into which we have entered. A key question raised by the proposals for a more nationalistic policy is whether or not the United States need involve itself in so many of the quarrels of the world?

When Dogs Quarrel — Should The Lion Care?

America is currently the dominant lion of the global arena. When the lesser animals quarrel, should the lion care?

On the plains of Africa, normally it does not. The lion rests while the hyenas yip noisily at one another. Only if the lion or its family is directly disturbed by the dogs does the lion take notice.

There is one situation in which the lion has to swat at the dogs — when a dog overreaches and snaps at the lion. Then it is sufficient for the lion to smash one dog hard for the others to learn to stay away.

This is a powerful metaphor for a nationalist policy.

Should the American lion allow itself to be drawn continually into quarrels among dogs? The answer is that generally it does not have to do so and may benefit greatly from not doing so. Yet, intervention in the quarrels of dogs has been the policy into which our cosmopolitan commitment has led us in the past seventy years.

Why does the American lion get into the quarrels of dogs all over the world? There are two reasons and both are bad.

First, the lion wants to control the dogs; so it intervenes everywhere. This was the course of the George W. Bush Administration.

Second, the lion wants to be a dog. It wants to be one of the pack — like everyone else. This is the course of the Obama Administration. It wants to be in the United Nations; it wants to participate in all the international agencies; it wants to lead from behind; it wants to be part of collective security agreements all over the globe.

The problem is that the lion is not a dog, and so it does not belong in the quarrels of the dogs. Everyone knows this except the delusional lion. So the dog which is the target of the lion's attention ordinarily backs away. When a dog stands its ground, the lion has to do all the heavy work of repressing it — the dogs which are on the lion's side give instructions and advice to the lion, but they do not help much. This is what happens with our allies and why collective security is largely an illusion for America (but not for America's allies).

We now have major arms build-ups going on in three places in the world, all major and critical:

Southeast and East Asia — sparked by Chinese militarization and outreach;
Middle East — sparked by Iran;
Russia — sparked by American and EU over-reach.

There is a growing danger of conflict in the regions of the three rising powers (China, Russia and Iran). In some senses it is like the emergence of the fascist powers before the Second World War — with armaments increasing in the Mediterranean and Africa around Italy; in Europe around Russia; and in Northeast Asia around Japan. The difference is that before World War II, America was not heavily armed and we were trying to ignore all this. When the dogs wanted to fight, the lion did not care. Now we are armed and trying to preserve the status quo, including peace, in all these regions simultaneously.

The American lion becomes frustrated and irritable at being continually involved in the quarrels of the dogs. It would be useful to try a different approach. This is what Trump proposes — a different approach.

Retiring The Western World Order

A different approach than cosmopolitanism is not difficult theoretically, but it may prove very difficult in practice. The American elite has propagated in America many illusions about the Western world order: that it will be accepted generally in the world; that we have the strength and influence to get it accepted; that promoting the Western world order will bring general peace and prosperity. These illusions have to be discarded and replaced with realistic expectations. The elites are likely in pursuit of their personal interests to resist vigorously any efforts to displace the Western world order from its primary position in American diplomacy.

But every year that passes demonstrates more clearly that the Western world order, whatever its theoretical advantages, is a dead letter in many of the most important parts of the globe. As this becomes more evident, the American electorate will recognize, without being told, the failure of diplomacy that seeks to impose the Western world order on a reluctant and resisting world. In this setting, it may be possible to disengage from illusion and pursue the realistic policy proposed in this book.

What The United States Stands For In The World — A Plea For Modesty

Americans like to say that people in other countries want the same things we want. Perhaps they do, at a basic human level. They want good food, comfortable and stylish clothing, a decent home, and safety. But they do not necessarily want what American cosmopolitans want at a political and cultural level. Americans like to say that the United

States stands for liberty, democracy and the rule of law. This seems good to Americans. But liberty, democracy and the rule of law are utilized in America to support a popular culture that stresses sex, drugs and violence. Since American cosmopolitans link these things inseparably, non-Americans often forge hostile attitudes toward the United States. Non-Americans do not necessarily want to tolerate aggressive religions and a popular culture of entertainment that focuses on materialism, drugs, sex and violence. Perhaps people of other nations should want these things. Many cosmopolitan Americans think freedom, acceptance and inclusion are the essence of modernity. Even Americans who object to materialism, drugs, sex and violence are remarkably unwilling to admit that these things dominate the nation's popular culture. But realism forces us to admit that these things seem to be being rejected in many parts of the world. Since materialism, drugs, sex and violence are inseparable in the cosmopolitan America with freedom, acceptance and inclusion, it is impossible for us to tell whether or not freedom, acceptance and inclusion have global appeal.

Focusing on the noble side of the American society, cosmopolitan Americans presume that others want such a society. Hence, Americans have a right to try to spread the American system worldwide. But the United States has no right to insist on the spread of its system if others don't want it — if others who may respect the ideals of the American system reject its results.

President Obama is fond of giving speeches abroad in which he candidly accepts serious shortcomings of the American system. Perhaps he doesn't realize that his modesty simply reinforces the aversion of many people abroad to the system which his policy seeks to spread worldwide.

The Post-Nation-State Era And The Failing Western Order

The world has been, until very recently, the province of the nation state — a circumstance given impetus by the reorganization of the world after the two world wars of the twentieth century. Then the wide empires of the British, French, Germans, Austrians and Turks were ended and nation states emerged in their wake.

The Western world order (now given primary sponsorship by the United States) endorses the nation state and prohibits any nation state from interfering by force with another nation state — in particular with national borders. For example, today the United States defends Ukraine from Russia; defends the nations of Southeast Asia against Chinese incursions in the disputed waters of the South China Sea; and defends Iraq and Syria from dismemberment by ISIL.

Defense of the nation state makes sense because the nation state is the best governing unit for democratically improving the social welfare of its citizens. It may not be a perfect unit, but it is better than any alternative with which we have experience.

But the dynamics of population growth, immigration and the politics of inclusiveness are weakening the nation state. A nation state is based on some unifying element among its population other than national borders — some commonality such as ethnicity or religion or culture. Lacking such, a state is merely a geographic area with a government. Today, as national coherence melts via immigration and cosmopolitan governments press the process, the reality of the nation state is being eroded in the West as it already has in much of the Middle East.

As the nation state turns into something else (a multi-ethnic immiscible battleground), the raison-d'être of the Western international political order erodes. Strong ties emerge among citizenry across international borders so that the sanctity of the nation state disappears; patriotism, including the willingness to defend a national homeland, dissipates; and American intervention on behalf of the Western world order with its emphasis on the nation state is ineffective and difficult to justify.

The individual country which is post-nation state increasingly appears as a failed state. It decays culturally and is without effective government. Failed states appear weak and vulnerable.

All that remains to protect the former nation states is American military power at home and abroad, and as American power declines in effectiveness, ambitious factions and nations become more aggressive. This is the dynamic that is occurring today. The remaining nation states, in particular Russia, China, Iran — each continuing to be cohesive via ethnicity, religion and culture — are tempted to extend their reach over various countries that are post-nation states, challenging America and the remnants of the EU.

Stabilizing The Middle East

Previous American administrations have helped create a tangle in the Middle East. So great is the mess that we cannot simply withdraw without unreasonably encouraging our Russian and Iranian rivals to greater ambitions. Hence, we need an exit plan now, after the bungled exits of the Bush and the Obama administrations, which led to the emergence of ISIS and the entry of Russian and Iranian forces into Syria and Iraq.

Such a plan would begin with the reoccupation of Iraq immediately before the Russians and Iranians have consolidated their hold (which will not be long from now). One or two American divisions will be needed. The ISIS-controlled area should be invaded and the leadership driven out. The most important thing is to accomplish this fully and quickly. It is much more important than trying to avoid the use of American troops.

Iraq should then be partitioned. A Kurdish country should be established; a Sunni country in the north and west of Iraq should be recognized; and a Shiite country should be recognized in the south of Iraq, which is likely to fall under Iranian control. We should squeeze the Russians who are based in Assad's strongholds and seek a political compromise.

In all human situations, how something is done is as important as what is done. In the Middle East, if America is to contain Russia's client Assad in Syria, it should not be done directly and announced, but done indirectly and without fanfare. This is what was very wrong with the petition of State Department employees announced on June 17, 2016, calling for direct American airstrikes to topple the Assad regime. Nothing of the sort should be done. Instead, the United States should destroy the Islamic State (ISIS) and in that process contain the Assad regime.

The borders of Syria and Iraq should be redrawn as necessary — neither need be left intact. With small weak states in what had been Iraq, Syria and Lebanon, we should expect Turkey and Israel and Iran and Saudi to dominate the region, rather as the Balkans are dominated by their larger neighbors. With the region in this condition, we should withdraw American troops for good. A significant degree of conflict will continue in the region; we need take no part in it. When dogs quarrel, the lion need not care.

We should expect that as all this is done, Russia will withdraw its troops from Syria, with the possible exception of its naval base on the Mediterranean. Assad can remain in his rump state of little Syria. Iran will have to reduce its ambitions in the region.

America should retain 10,000 or so troops in Afghanistan to preserve a favorably-oriented government and to retain a position on Iran's eastern side. American troops in Afghanistan would also help to reduce the Chinese influence in Afghanistan.

There is no need to seek coalitions to support us in these things. We have to accomplish our purposes ourselves. But in each instance we should accept very-interested allies (Israel, Egypt and Saudi in Mesopotamia; India in Afghanistan). We should consult and pay attention to affected powers (such as Turkey, Britain, and France) in how we do things, as in forming a Kurdish state, but we must be prepared to do things over their objections if necessary. We should smile at the rest of the world, including the international organizations (like President Franklin D. Roosevelt used to do) but leave them out.

In other words, the United States should act. We should reenter the vacuum that still exists in the Middle East from our recent departure and do it now and then reorder the region in geo-strategic terms to our liking, and then in a few years, slowly withdraw.

A Cold-Peace With Russia

The American effort to reset our relationship with Russia to a partnership has been a resounding failure. The causes have been excellently analyzed by Steven Rosefielde in *Kremlin Strikes Back: Russia and the*

West after Crimea's Annexation and several other books and articles. We are now entangled in a second Cold War that Washington intermittently acknowledges and denies.

What America should do is to move from Cold War II toward a Cold Peace so that the risk of open conflict is much reduced.

The goal is modest because of cosmopolitan America's mistaken conviction that Russia is weak prevents the American presidency from sanely managing the relationship. In other words, it is because American leaders wrongly believe that they can and will prevail unilaterally on their terms. There is ample scope for compromise; it is worth exploring to reduce the risk of conflagration, but "normalization" under current circumstances is not tantamount to renewed hegemonic American partnership. We have walked into in a perilous situation because our policymakers refuse to face new realities, believing that they can always tough things out. We now need to make our way carefully out of danger.

Hope For The Future

There is hope that the United States will do a much better job in its international role in the near future. This hope arises out of a major change that is about to occur in our national leadership as a result of the presidential election of 2016.

It appears that the United States is finally preparing to depart from its decades-long pattern of electing to the presidency young and inexperienced people who are characterized by good looks and idealistic rhetoric. Whether these young people are Democrat or Republican they lack the good judgment which comes with knowledge and experience and too often behave like political entrepreneurs. Information is available much more readily than before, but information is not knowledge (which requires a framework for comprehension and analysis), nor judgment (which requires experience). A more seasoned president will help America to cease foundering in our efforts abroad.

Chapter 3

Key Elements Of An American Policy For Today

In this chapter, we propose a very specific policy for the United States. Our effort responds to a continual demand made in the election campaign for specificity about alternatives to the current Administration's policies. Trump has been understandably reticent in responding to these demands since they are made by his political enemies and with no other purpose than to find additional grounds on which to attack him.

We are specific in our proposals. There are many courses of action which make sense for America; there are only a few which are deeply-mistaken. The American government has been on a deeply-mistaken course. Our specific recommendations do not mean that we think these are the only courses of action which make sense for America, but they are among the best.

The eleven points below should be the key elements of American policy strategy. The eleven points are accompanied by six characteristics and eleven principles of policy which will be cited in subsequent chapters.

The strategy below should be a basis for a return to a bipartisan policy in America. All eleven points are departures to some degree from current American policy — although the confusion and internal contradictions of current American policy may make this unclear. In some instances, the points below are substantial departures from current policy — as especially with respect to Russia, the Middle East and the European Union.

Summarizing The World Situation

It is useful to briefly characterize the world in which we must conduct our policy. It is surprisingly easy to describe its most significant characteristics and it is surprisingly little done in the continual discussion that occurs in the American media and professional literature.

There are seven principal regions of the world. Four have similar aggregate populations. The world's total population is some 7.3 billion people.

The West	1.4 billion people
Russia	0.1 billion people
Islam	1.4 billion people
China	1.4 billion people
India	1.4 billion people
Africa south of the Sahara	1.0 billion people
Southeast Asia and Japan	0.6 billion people
Total population	7.3 billion people

The four largest regions identified above can each be considered a geo-political bloc. Two are single enormous nations (China and India). Two are made up of multiple nations (The West — and Islam) but have strong internal linkages. Russia is geographically a major bloc in itself (about one-seventh of the Earth's land area), though it is much smaller than the other blocs in population (about 143 million, rounded off in the table to 100 million). It is, of course, a nation state. The final two of the seven are mini-blocs, each made up of many nations and without strong internal linkages. At this moment, although the West is engaged in internal dissention involving Russia's role and Islam is engaged in internal dissention between Shia and Sunnis, none of the largest regions (the West, Islam, China and India) are in external danger. Africa south of the Sahara and Southeast Asia are both subject to pressures from outside powers that might disrupt them, pulling elements of them into the orbit of one of the four major powers.

The most important fact in world politics today is that each of the four major blocs is currently aggressive, as is Russia. Each is trying to expand its control or influence geographically. The West is trying to spread the Western world-order worldwide. Russia is trying to expand in Eastern Europe. China is trying to expand into the South China Sea. India continues to try to consolidate Kashmir. Islam is trying to expand its reach into Europe, Africa south of the Sahara, and North America (the United States and Canada). The means for expansion differ. The West uses political methods (the so-called "color revolutions," for example), followed by military consolidation (inclusion in NATO or some other military alliance). Russia uses political subversion and military force. China uses military power in the South China Sea. India uses military force in Kashmir and in the Indian Ocean. Islam uses population movement (either refugees or immigrants) and quasi-military force (terrorist units).

In summary, we have a world divided into competing blocs, the most important of which are trying to expand, often against each another.

Our purpose is to propose an American policy for this world configuration.

Eleven Points For American Policy

The eleven points are in the following order:

- The first deals with Russia because it is the most potentially dangerous of our rivals;
- The second deals with Iran and Islamism because they are currently the most active of our antagonists;
- The third through the eighth deal with China and its neighbors because it is an increasingly aggressive rival;
- The ninth deals with the European Union because it is an increasingly uncertain ally;

- The tenth deals with a source of potential trouble in the Western Hemisphere; and
- The eleventh deals with our trade policies which undercut our nation's economic strength.

1. Seek a Cold Peace with Russia, rather than the second Cold War which is now being decried by many observers. We should allow Russia to resist the further extension of NATO and the European Union into Eastern Europe and the former states of the Soviet Union. This is appropriate at a time when Russia has largely effective leadership and when it is rearming aggressively. We should join Russia in efforts to contain China. Russia isn't going to partner with America for this purpose while America is engaged in a new Cold War against the Kremlin on multiple levels. We should bolster Russia outside the Middle East by accepting a Russian sphere of influence in much of what was the Soviet Union — in order that Russia may assist us in helping to contain China and in helping to restrain radical Islam. If a Cold Peace can be achieved, then we should seek a reduction in the pace of military modernization (20 percent per annum 2010–2015) being pursued by Russia so that there is less chance of a major war in the coming decade.

2. Contain Iranian ambitions in order to weaken a rival and preserve our access to another critical region of the globe. This requires rescinding the Iran Nuclear Agreement. Officially, American policy should involve stick and carrot soft containment. Act to restrain Iran while simultaneously promoting partnership.

3. Accept a restructuring of national borders in the Middle East by

   i. working out new borders in conjunction with Russia and the European Union. As a practical matter, a partition of Syria and Iraq is already underway;
   ii. establishing a Kurdish state by negotiated settlement;
   iii. accepting a sphere of influence for Iran in what remnant remains of Iraq, which presumably will be a Shia enclave; and

iv. accepting that this arrangement need not be stable — a degree of chaos is tolerable, as long as our enemies are kept weak and America is a much lessened target of radical Islam. The United States should seek not final victory but division and weakness among our enemies.

4. Contain China in order to restrain a rival and preserve our access to a critical region of the globe. What is required is a stick and carrot soft containment. Hard military containment is not yet needed and probably is unachievable. We should therefore act via military restraint while simultaneously promoting partnership. But we must be very careful not to stumble into war. China is moving aggressively to increase its military, economic and political influence in Southeast Asia. When Japan did this in the early 1940s, American opposition to Japan's ambitions precipitated World War II. A key reason was that the United States strongly opposed Japan's move, but appeared disunited and vacillating. The Japanese misread their American rival and interpreted America as weak. They turned to force as a way to resist the American opposition. We are now sending similar signals to China in a closely analogous situation. Though neither the United States nor China at this point wants open hostilities, we risk stumbling into war in two primary ways.

First, via an unintended clash of naval forces in the South China Sea.

Second, via a determination by China that the United States can be forced out of the region by force (the same miscalculation made by Japan in 1941).

5. Strengthen Japan in order to help restrain China.

6. Strengthen India in order to help restrain China.

7. Support ASEAN (the association of Southeast Asian nations) in order to help restrain China.

8. Cooperate with Thailand, Myanmar, Cambodia, and Vietnam while softening democracy-promoting sanctions against these countries. China is more important than wrist-slapping potential allies.

9. Permit the European Union to evolve in whatever direction works out — even if it falls apart. During the current developing turmoil occasioned by the immigration crisis and by the debt crisis in southern Europe, work to contain any instability within its current borders. If the European Union breaks up, try to have friendly relations with each of the emerging national entities. Resist German efforts to continue the advance of NATO and the EU east into what Russia considers its sphere of influence — at least so long as Russia is firmly led, as it is now by Vladimir Putin. In the current context, Germany isn't leading the advance of NATO and the EU to the east, but instead is egging on the United States to provoke the Russians while Germany publicly refuses to fight in Ukraine. It is exactly this sort of abuse of the American military umbrella which is calling into disrepute in America the cosmopolitan policy pursued since the Second World War.

10. Discretely support political freedom in Venezuela and Cuba, and thereby restrain a source of potential trouble in the Americas. Trump's actions must be discrete because a brash policy will backfire.

11. Alter our trade policies to seek to maintain and reestablish high-wage good-producing companies. Seek also to strengthen our middle-sized firms. Provide no implicit subsidies (including via regulations) for Wall Street driven globalization. Finally, do our best to keep a significant lead in high technology businesses, not the least by refusing to allow their sale to rival powers. We could do much worse than emulate Germany's economic policies in these regards. American policy, whatever its public rationale, has had the effect of exporting our manufacturing with its high compensation, working and middle class jobs. It has also greatly strengthened our large global, publicly-listed firms at the expense of all other sectors of our economy. If this proposal is criticized as an "industrial policy" in which the government would pick winners and losers, the answer is that we already have an industrial policy (no matter how much both Democratic and Republican administrations deny it) in which the government creates

winners and losers, and it is one that has impoverished the American working and middle classes.

The Risk Of Our Current Course: Provoking Our Rivals To War

Major wars are virtually unavoidable if the United States follows its current geo-political course and does not have a substantial preponderance of power. Since we are currently giving ground in the correlation of forces to our major rivals — Russia, China and Iran — war is becoming increasingly likely.

America seems determined to deny the international aspirations of our rivals, so that each is likely to turn to force when it feels strong enough. This is why American strength is so important. War can only be avoided by the United States having such a preponderance of power that our rivals are deterred from acting. It is fatal for us to act as if there will not be war — as if economic ties or peaceful intentions alone can prevent conflict — and then stumble into war.

It was exactly this sort of ill-considered American policy that led us into the Pearl Harbor disaster in 1941. We denied Japan its aspirations in China, but didn't prepare for war. We seemed to think that Japan would not resort to war, although it was well-armed and belligerent (as are Russia, China and Iran today). The Japanese had defeated the Russians in 1903, and easily conquered the Chinese in the 1930s. Therefore, we had no grounds for complacency in 1941. Japan did resort to war and we were its target.

It is useful to note here that the important analogy for today from the 1930s is not appeasement of Germany, but instead confrontation with Japan without sufficient military power backing us. We are doing something similar again.

The major objection to the current drift of cosmopolitan American policy — which is actually bi-partisan — is that it is certain to lead to major war. We are provoking our rivals greatly while reducing our military strength to back up our positions. This invites our rivals to test us militarily.

We should also recognize that we are not certain to win any future military challenge. Unfortunately, we may lose a war because our government appears corrupt, incompetent and self-deluded.

We need not have so much military strength if our policy is more accommodating to one or more of our major rivals, so that the challenges we face are of lesser degree. In later chapters we will make a case for this direction of policy.

Chapter 4

The Six Characteristics Of A Desirable Policy For America

A merican policy should be:

- Complete,
- Comprehensive,
- Coherent,
- Consistent,
- Credible, and
- Compliant.

Specifically, these characteristics mean:

Complete

A complete policy is thorough. It is not partial and incomplete. Nothing of importance is left out. It does not deal with different topics and different regions of the world as if they were separate topics for separate policies. It does not compartmentalize except for the application of the broad strategy of the overall policy (that is, for tactics).

Comprehensive

A comprehensive policy is wide-ranging because America's concerns in the world are wide-ranging. Economic, military, social and political concerns are all included.

Coherent

A coherent policy makes sense to us and to others. It is clear, not muddled; it can be explained in a logical manner; it has well-defined and generally accepted (within America) objectives and means which can reasonably be expected to achieve the objectives. It appears to be reasoned and well-thought-out.

Consistent

The elements of a consistent policy are properly aligned to support each other instead of to work at cross-purposes. As we shall see below, there are many and major inconsistencies in our policy now which are a significant source of its failures.

Credible

A credible policy must be believable to both us and our rivals. We, the people, are more gullible than our adversaries. We as an electorate are prepared to accept elements of wishful thinking and idealism as part of a credible policy. Our adversaries are not. Hence it is necessary for our policy to be realistic and devoid of wishful thinking and idealistic distortion if it is to be credible abroad. Our current policy is full of both wishful thinking and deluded idealism. It is viewed in Europe as hypocritical; in Asia as foolish; in the rest of the world as a strange affectation of the Americans. Nowhere is it taken seriously except where it leads to conflict and other unnecessary evils. No one sees a gain for themselves is pointing out to us the incredibility of our present policies; so they humor us. As the proverb goes, answer a fool in the language of his foolishness, as all nations do answer us now, and that fool will believe himself wise — as the America establishment now believes itself to be wise.

Compliant

A policy must be compliant because the world is always changing. It must be adjusted to these changes as required. The art, of course, is to change it only when it is necessary — not to adopt a frivolous flexibility. The art is also not to be so rigid that stubbornness replaces an informed and intelligent compliance.

Chapter 5

Underlying Principles Of An American Policy

Twelve principles of strategy underlie the specifics of the policy which are detailed above. We begin with the basic principle of nationalism, which is the topic of this book. America should:

1. Build Policy Strictly On The Principle Of Core National Interest — Not Insider Interest Nor Domestic Politics

This is the basic principle of nationalism. It subordinates international goals, however idealistic, to national interest, just as it subordinates the interests of other nations (even those of our allies), and of private groups, corporations and individuals. The moral argument for this approach is that our nation is an extended family, and every member of a family has the responsibility to care for the other members of the family first.

2. Work For These Objectives Diplomatically; We Should Resort To Force Only If Necessary — That Is, For Defense Against Armed Aggression

3. Engage Only One Major Adversary At A Time, Not All Potential Adversaries At Once

This is an important principle even if we think we are strong enough to engage all at once. It is a principle of caution. It encourages us to work to separate our opponents and turn them against one another, rather than to unite them against us and simply try to out-weigh them in a contest.

We should not try to block the aspirations of Russia, China and Iran all at the same time. We are not strong enough to prevail in the longer-term if they unite against us. So, we should not give them cause to unite against us. Divide and prevail is a key principle of conflict which we should honor. We can prevail if we don't try to do too much at once.

Because we have violated this principle, Russia, China and Iran have put their rivalries on the back-burner and focus on needling the United States. They can pursue their own interests doing complementary things that weaken Western influence and make them jointly less vulnerable to Western sanctions. That is what they are doing. The situation is analogous to the interwar years. Germany, Italy and Japan were potential rivals, but it would have been foolish for them to fail to cooperate when they faced common adversaries — Britain, France, the Soviet Union and the United States.

Today, Russia provides a western theater of engagement; China provides an eastern theater; and Iran provides a southern theatre. All three need to be considered in one overall strategic conception, but managed as independent problems even though some policies may be jointly effective. Russia, China and Iran each seek to expand spheres of influence in their immediate neighborhoods. Containing one of them doesn't contain the other.

4. Promote Beneficial Government Abroad, Not Our Form Of Democracy

We should abandon our advocacy of a Western-style world order and accept a multi-polar and diverse world. We should endorse good government in whatever form it is found. That is, if the people of another nation are benefitting economically and socially, then we should applaud that. We should abandon our focus on governmental processes and endorse favorable results instead. We should abandon our conviction that the key matters are institutions and procedures — a notion we get from our law which focuses on process and not results — and endorse good results for populations abroad from whatever system generates them.

5. Quit Appearing On The International Stage As If We Were No More Than Platitude-Spouting Hypocrites

Our politicians continually wrap our policy objectives and actions in moral terms. The result is that most perceptive foreigners see our leaders of both political parties as platitude-mouthing hypocrites. American politicians take a moralistic tack because the American people respond positively to the notion that America is especially good. In some ways we are. In others we are not. The inconsistency between our pretensions and our actions undermines our reputation in the world.

6. Assert Our National Interests In Preference To Those Of Other Nations

The governing cosmopolitan elite of the United States began in the aftermath of World War II to concern itself with the well-being of other nations as an objective of American policy. This was to gain allies in the Cold War. The orientation of the United States on behalf of other countries' welfare has now been carried so far that to many, possibly most, Americans it appears that our government is on the side of other nations rather than on our own. Too much of the welfare of the American people has been sacrificed to insiders in other countries. Abroad, this is viewed not as American generosity, but as either American confusion or corruption. We should be like other countries and pursue our own interests. The old Cold War is over, and there is now no advantage to be gained for our country by sacrificing our own interests.

7. Conduct Any Foreign Interventions Well, Including Having An Exit Strategy And Using It

The United States should not get entangled in problems that it cannot competently resolve. We can design intervention forces as a bluff, but should not meddle. The Obama Administration's support for color revolutions in the Middle East demonstrates the danger in meddling. When it is necessary to involve ourselves militarily abroad, then we should do it well. We should get in when necessary and get out as soon as possible. We should avoid getting stuck in quicksand. When we squash a danger to us, we do not have to fix everything else in the affected region. We can leave chaos in our wake if that is what emerges. Once the immediate objective is attained, American forces should be withdrawn. Leaving chaos behind is not the worst thing; and trying to rebuild nations in the western model is likely to fail. So we should get out when the immediate objective is accomplished. If danger to us reappears, we can go in and squash it again. This is an intelligent and cost-effective use of our power. Anything else is romantic — the notion that we can set the world to right. We can't.

8. Keep Our Eyes On The Major Things And Do Not Get Distracted

A key element of leadership is to do a few critically important things well and avoid distractions that might prevent this. American leaders need to do the same thing. Today, the most important thing is to avoid a full-scale conflict with the Russians, who are as well armed with nuclear weapons as we are; the second and third most important things are to contain the Chinese and prevail against radical Islam. If these three things are accomplished, America will be safe and secure. If they are not accomplished — or if even one is not done — then we will be in great difficulty. Nothing else matters if we cannot get these three things done. There are potentially many different ways to accomplish these things; our challenge is to choose means and proceed to accomplish our purpose. To be specific, we can ally ourselves with Russia, agreeing that it can strengthen itself to a degree; or we can attempt to block its re-assertiveness. We are now trying to block Russia's re-assertiveness — which is much riskier than accepting Russia as a legitimate great power.

We can disengage with radical Islam, or we can move to crush it. We are trying to crush it without much success. If we rely on our new, though expensive, supply of oil and also on new non-carbon energy sources in order to disengage from the region, we will likely find that radical Islam loses interest in us.

We can attempt to contain China within its current region, or we can permit it to dominate the South China Sea. If we cede dominance in the Far East to China, we may be able to retain economic access to the region. This is a likely approach for a Clinton Administration; a Trump administration is more likely to attempt to contain China within its current range.

These are America's major choices and we shouldn't allow concerns such as support for Palestinian claims against Israel, climate change, refugees, etc., to interfere.

9. We Should Never Lose Sight Of Our Most Dangerous Potential Adversary

Over time America's most dangerous potential adversary changes. For the first half of the twentieth century our most dangerous potential adversary was Germany. In the seventy years since our most dangerous potential adversary has been Russia (whether as the Soviet Union or as Russia). This is because Russia is so powerfully armed with nuclear weapons. With today's Russian re-assertiveness (including Russia's announcement that it is now developing a next generation of nuclear weapons), Russia is almost certain to remain our most dangerous potential adversary. In consequence, we must keep the Russians foremost in our sight. Perhaps in a decade the greater potential danger will be the Chinese. Militant Islam is not a potentially most dangerous adversary. It is simply the most troublesome. At the present, we must not denigrate the Russians — they are the only foreign power able to obliterate us. When Putin reminds us of this, we should take him seriously. Denouncing him, as so many of our politicians seem to delight in doing, is playing with fire.

10. Be Clear About Our Objectives, Not Muddle-Headed

We need to make clear to ourselves (for we are a large, complex and diverse nation) and to our allies the key elements of our policy in order that our people and others can support us and help accomplish our goals. If we decide to obliterate radical Islam, we should say so clearly and send in our troops to do so. If we decide to contain China and deny it a sphere of influence in East Asia, then we should say so, and place the necessary naval forces in the South China Sea. If we decide to deny Russia an enlarged sphere of influence, we should say so clearly and place the necessary forces in Eastern Europe. America has a history of not making clear its policy objectives, or of not making them credible by deploying the force necessary to attain them. President Obama has concealed key policy objectives since he has been concerned that they will not be popular in the United States. By concealing key objectives, he has completely confused our people, our allies and our potential opponents. In some areas of the world he seems to have had no objectives (other than to cope with events), so he has left our allies leaderless.

11. Do Not Compartmentalize Too Much

It is often observed that we have a global economy. We recognize that economic events in one part of the world impact other parts. We sometimes recognize that the impact is significant, even determinative in the economic sphere. Yet in policy we seem to often treat various theatres of the world as distinctly separate. We over-compartmentalize.

In fact, every major national power is concerned to some degree, sometimes a very large degree, in all areas of the world. An event in an apparently isolated area can be of great concern elsewhere. Major powers, who joust with each other on a global basis, get involved openly or behind the scenes all over the world. Hence it was that the Soviet Union got involved in Cuba during the Cold War, causing us considerable discomfort there, far from Eurasia's shores.

12. Be Prepared To Pay For Power

America seems not to want to pay for power. America received world hegemony at no cost when the USSR collapsed. The United States was vaulted from the position of one of two superpowers engaged in the Cold War into the position of the world's single superpower able to influence virtually everything in the world. Over the next 25 years our government missed opportunities and misused its power to the extent that now it has to pay to keep it. As former Secretary of Defense Bob Gates put the choice, "America can have either world power or a welfare state. It cannot have both." The election of 2016 will be the first test of the desire of Americans to retain power and the first test of our willingness to pay for it.

Summary Of Underlying Principles

- Build policy strictly on the principle of core national interest; not insider interest and tactical domestic politics.
- Work for these objectives diplomatically; we should resort to force only when made necessary by defense against armed aggression.
- Engage only one major adversary at a time, not all potential adversaries at once.
- Promote beneficial government abroad, not simply our own form of democracy.
- Quit appearing on the international stage as if we are no more than platitude-spouting hypocrites.
- Assert our national interests in preference to those of other nations.
- Conduct any foreign interventions well, including having an exit strategy.

- Keep our eyes on the major things and do not get distracted.
- Never lose sight of our most dangerous potential adversary.
- Be clear about our objectives, not muddle-headed.
- Do not compartmentalize too much.
- Be prepared to pay for power.

Chapter 6

More About The Most Important Principles Of A Successful Policy

Of the principles identified in the previous chapter, several will benefit from further discussion.

Number 3. Engage Only One Major Adversary At A Time, Not All Potential Adversaries At Once

It is foolish to oppose the aspirations of all other major powers at the same time because that invites them to combine against us. But cosmopolitan America is now doing this.

A very significant example of the danger we are courting by our current foreign policy is given by the announcement in late July, 2016, that China will join Russia in joint naval exercises in the South China Sea. This drill continues a pattern of naval cooperation in the area which was initiated a few years ago. Though China insists the exercises are purely peaceful, they also come as China has rejected a finding of an international arbitration panel in Europe that China has no rights to portions of the South China Sea in which it is building military bases.

There are only two possible explanations as to why the United States persists in opposing the aspirations of all its major rivals simultaneously. Either:

1. We Americans believe we have such a preponderance of power that even should all potential adversaries unite against us, we would readily prevail; or
2. We believe our potential adversaries' own aspirations are not significant to them, but that instead we are engaged in the kind of exclusively verbal debate which occurs continually within a democracy and which is not the kind of controversy which causes warfare; that is, that this is a verbal debate not a serious conflict of interests.

Neither of these two explanations appears likely.

First, we lack such a preponderance of power that we can readily dispose of combinations against us. This is true whatever sorts of power — tactical hard, strategic hard or cyber — or international political influence are considered. Periodically, American politicians of each major party declare that America possesses overwhelming military power.

The assertion by politicians of American military power is usually accompanied by the assertion that the United States spends more on the military each year than any other combination of nations. This is almost certainly a result of the underreporting of military spending abroad. Also, much American military spending is disguised social programs — efforts to expand racial and gender equality, environmental protection, anti-drug enforcement, etc. The result is that American military power is not what official statistics suggest. Further, and most important, we now face several weapons systems which we have not faced before — including especially cyber force — so that the effectiveness of our forces in action is now uncertain.

Second, each of our major potential adversaries is currently demonstrating that its national aspiration is worthy of military action:

Russia in Crimea and Ukraine
China in the South China Sea
Iran in Iraq via formal military forces and in Iraq and elsewhere in
    the Middle East via terrorism.

But American military and political strength, however inadequate at this point, might be increased until we once again have the power to oppose all potential adversaries at once. What is more important is our will to prevail and the commitment to pay the price, for the will determines whether or not we develop the power to resist any or all adversaries; and the will determines whether or not we use the force we have. It is not clear that America has the will to resist the ambitions of other powers, particularly if it becomes clear that resistance involves politically sensitive cost.

What is clear is that it is likely that having the will to prevail means that the cost of resistance can be very much minimized. This is because most often an aggressive hostile power gains strength until it is stopped, so that the earlier it is stopped, the less strength it is able to employ in its aggressive efforts. The less strength an aggressor is able to employ, the less it will cost America to thwart it.

The general position of the authors of this book is simple and direct. It is that the United States should accommodate if possible (as we did the United Kingdom in the later 19th century), and defeat if necessary (as we did Germany in the early 20th century).

The major powers at the moment ranked by strategic power are Russia, China, Iran and Germany.

As political forces in the world, the major powers can be summarized as follows: Russia is opportunistic; China is assertive; Iran is ambitious; Germany is devious.

Currently, short-term American priorities are in this order: Iran, Russia, China, and Germany.

The reason is that Islamic terrorism is killing Americans now; it is creating hysteria in the United States; so it seems that it must be answered in some form immediately.

But, as we will explain later, this is an error. Russia should currently be at the top of America's priority list.

Russia is well armed with fifth generation hardware and has the nuclear power to destroy us, but it is not an immediate threat of war, unless by accident. China is not as serious a threat as Russia at the moment, but is becoming more militarily aggressive and so must be responded to at some point; Germany seems currently largely pacifist and so to most Americans seems no problem.

It is impossible to ascertain the longer-term priorities of the current American Administration.

Longer-term American priorities should be in a somewhat different order: China, Russia, Germany, Iran. This is because China has more long-term military and political potential than Russia; and because Germany has the potential to rival us globally; even to defeat us. Iran does not.

Number 4. Promote Beneficial Government

Americans think too much like attorneys. We tend to focus on process and not on results. We have been stressing the Western world order as a one-size-fits-all prescription for other countries in the world. Some countries our prescription fits; many it does not. Those countries are resisting and it is evident that at this time the Western world order is being rejected in the other major powers of the world, with the exception of the European Union and its German leader.

This situation holds the potential for unnecessary conflict.

The United States should cease to promote the Western world order everywhere, as it now does, and instead should support beneficial government wherever it appears and in whatever form. This is a results-oriented prescription, not a process-oriented prescription.

The essence of democracy as explained in Rosefielde and Mills, *Democracy and its Elected Enemies* is the frequent and peaceful transfer of power via an honest election. If that basic requirement is followed in a foreign country, then the United States should support it as a fellow democracy. Other than that, each democracy should be allowed to follow its own processes.

Further, where democracies create beneficial governments — by improving economic conditions, raising living and health standards, promoting peace in the nearby region, etc. — America should be supportive. Beneficial government, conceived this way, should be America's objective abroad, not the Western world order.

The world is continually producing necessary changes. This may include some international borders. The best example at the moment involves borders in the Middle East in which the borders Syria, Iraq, Saudi Arabia, Kuwait, Lebanon and Jordan were created largely by the Western powers after World War I with little reference to local conditions. It may now be necessary to a lasting peace that these borders be adjusted, even in some instances over opposition. Yet America has anointed itself the world's guardian of established borders.

It is necessary that our country abandon our insistence on the sanctity of all international borders and our role as defender of the status quo which is implicit in America as the world's policeman of international law.

What is being recommended here is a rule of judgment where a rule of endorsement has prevailed. We should support beneficial government instead of supporting particular democratic procedures. We should accept changes in international borders when necessary to pacification in a region, not merely insist on the sanctity of any borders which currently exist.

Number 6. Assert Our National Interests In Preference To Those Of Other Nations

Is there any evidence that we have more global peace for the present United States policy of internationalist cosmopolitanism? In fact, it is exactly the opposite — instead of more peace we have a descent of the world into increasing conflict.

If the notion is that favoring other nations promotes peace, where is the evidence? It is not found in history. For example, there is peace in North America between Canada and the United States and between Mexico and the United States, but it is not because of good will, but because the preponderance of power is so strongly in favor of the United States that war is not conceivable. Before the preponderance of power was established, there was war between the United States and Canada and between the United States and Mexico.

Many Americans have a different view. They buy into the notion that integrated economies and therefore having a lot to lose economically is the best way to minimize conflict. This notion they prefer to the explanation of a preponderance of power.

This notion is a more attractive one than preponderance of power. It stresses the good in humanity. It is believed by many of its adherents not because there is evidence of it, but because it is something they prefer to believe. It is more comforting. It is a form of wishful-thinking, which is something at which many people are very good.

Unfortunately, there is little or no evidence supporting it. As a single example, World War I broke out at the time that the world economy was at its most integrated in history (up to that point). In fact, again and again in history, international political ambitions have triumphed over any economic or financial considerations.

Nothing in the trade relationships of today is of the nature to prevent nations drifting close to or into war. This is unfortunate — we would much prefer that the opposite to be true — but it is realistic.

Our purpose is to propose a policy which avoids wars, especially large scale war. The issue is how. Economic integration helps; it provides an interest group for peace — those who profit from international economic exchange. For economic integration to be successful in avoiding war, it requires that those who benefit most from economic integration — in today's world, businesses that sell or buy in international markets, or finance, or governments that tax trade — should have the political influence to prevail against others for whom war may be desirable for one reason or another. This is a matter of political happenstance. Hence, it cannot be relied upon as a sure method of avoiding war.

Preponderance of power is a sure method of avoiding war so long as two conditions exist:

1. The nation with the preponderance of power does not use it to so oppress others that war breaks out despite desperate odds against those who rebel; and
2. The preponderance of power is not subject to doubt, so that nations are tempted to test the strength of the greatest power.

In the world today, America does not oppress its potential rivals, so there is no danger there. But American power is now subject to doubt on many bases including the will to use it, technological superiority (especially cyber-power), actual magnitude, etc. Because American preponderance of power is subject to doubt, the danger of war is substantial. Because America gives little evidence of being willing to restore its preponderance of power, the danger of war will continue, and we must consider how best to avoid war. This is an underlying reason why cosmopolitanism is now outdated and why a shift in American policy toward a more national orientation is advisable.

Number 7. Conduct Any Foreign Interventions Well, Including Having An Exit Strategy

Historically, America has two major approaches to military interventions abroad:

- Limited objectives (to live with the opponent);
- Unlimited objectives (to destroy/subjugate the opponent).

The Revolution, the undeclared war against France, and the War of 1812 were fought for limited objectives. In conducting those conflicts we understood that we would, in the future, live with our opponents. We sought to defeat them, not dismember or otherwise destroy them. We did not seek to change their regimes.

The Mexican War, the Civil War, the Spanish-American War, and the First and Second World Wars were fought for unlimited objectives — to subordinate the enemy to our will — unconditional surrender, in effect. We fought to change the regimes of these countries and in some cases to dismember our opponents.

In the modern period, the Korean War, Vietnam and the first Iraq War were fought for limited objectives.

The Afghan War and the Second Iraq War were fought for unlimited objectives.

It is crucial to be clear about our purpose when we resort to military interventions. Is a conflict for limited or unlimited purposes? It is common for us to disagree about this in recent conflicts. Many Americans criticize President George H. W. Bush for pursuing only limited objectives (which were attained) in the First Iraqi War.

Disaster can result when objectives are not clear. President George W. Bush initiated the Second Iraqi War for the purpose of disposing of the Saddam Hussein regime. But when this limited objective was accomplished, the President imposed a major new purpose — to build a modern state in Iraq. This was the source of the long, unsatisfactory conflict which has followed.

What was needed at the end of the Saddam Hussein regime was a plan for the withdrawal of American forces from Iraq. If one existed, it was not put into effect at that time. Always, limited objective military interventions must be accompanied from the outset with plans, political and military, for exit — otherwise the intervention will become what Iraq and Afghanistan have become — tar pits of American policy.

Number 8. Keep Our Eyes On The Major Things

Errors play a critical role in international politics; they often shape the future and provide the raw material for conflict. We must try to eliminate causes of major errors. Among the most important causes is a failure to keep our attention on the major aspects of an international situation.

Examples are numerous since world events are much simpler in origin than intellectuals can ordinarily accept. The most important is probably the mistake of geo-politics which invited World War II. It arose as so many American mistakes do, out of the idealistic application of a moral principle to the world of realpolitik. The principle was articulated by the American President Woodrow Wilson as one of self-determination of ethnic groups. The Poles, the Czechs, the Hungarians, and southern Slavs were all to have their own nations. To create these nations, the Western democracies after World War I dismantled the great European empires — the Austrian Empire, the Russian Empire, and the Turkish Empire. But they left Germany essentially intact bordered in the east by small nations which could not defend themselves against Germany. Thus, Germany was free to reassert itself in more a favorable environment. The result was World War II.

It is common for the American media and many of our pundits to take their eyes off the big threats, which have been latent, and to become caught in their own myopia. A mistake in Iraq can be redeemed over time. A mistake in Ukraine or in the South China Sea could be fatal.

America cannot avoid having to respond to challenges of a less than mortal nature — that is challenges offered by lesser powers. To attempt to do so would be to try to impose a policy regime which would deserve the criticism that it is a warmed-over isolationism.

Instead, we stress the importance of setting policies for less important situations in an integrated global framework that allows us to shift resources rationally across our national agenda.

Number 11. Do Not Compartmentalize Too Much

Over-compartmentalization is a major failing of the American approach to policy. It seems to be a habit of the American mind. We seem to wish to see each challenge as its own and independent of other influences. If the problem is resolved, fairytale style, everyone lives happily ever after. Perhaps this avoids complications which would arise from multiple causalities. Perhaps it would also confuse our democratic dialogue in which the majority of the electorate is necessarily largely ignorant of nuances and complications and impatient with them. The result is that we do not ordinarily accurately assess the challenges we face.

A few examples are in order. We found it difficult to believe that the Korean War was strategically (though not operationally) directed from Moscow, and that so was the Vietnam War. The Soviet Union employed proxy powers against us in both these wars. We seem to have preferred the more direct approach of our German and Japanese enemies of the World War II period — neither Germany nor Japan employed proxy states against us. This is not to say that the proxies did not have certain interests of their own, and even some degree of independence from their backers. But America would have crushed the North Koreans quickly without their Soviet backers (who authorized the Chinese to enter the war), and would have crushed the North Vietnamese quickly without their Soviet backers.

Perhaps our habit of compartmentalization was strengthened by our experience in World War II, in which we fought disconnected wars in Europe and the Pacific, and so got accustomed to only regional threats. But while neither Germany nor Japan was then able to act on a global basis, Russia and China today are able to act on a global basis, and surprisingly, Iran may also be able to do so. The result is that events in different portions of the globe are likely to be intimately connected.

American presidents have sometimes reacted appropriately to global threats — that is to threats in one region of the globe that are coordinated centrally. These presidents have responded to non-compartmentalized challenges by acting outside the compartments. But American political opponents of those presidents have always condemned our presidents for such actions and have ordinarily prevailed with American public opinion. The most important example is that John F. Kennedy decided to intervene in Vietnam to show the Soviet premier, Nikita Khrushchev, that America would stand up to the Soviet Union. Most Americans found this impossible to accept then and still do.

Chapter 7

Seizing Opportunities And Avoiding Entangling Alliances

America Should Seize Opportunities To Secure The Future

American diplomatic history in recent decades is full of lost opportunities. The United States must cease wasting its chances to improve the future.

The greatest lost opportunity was to build a secure relationship with Russia. The collapse of the Soviet Union in 1991 offered this opportunity. The United States could have helped prevent or mitigate the drastic economic collapse which then occurred in Russia. It could have helped build secure borders for the remnant of the Soviet Union that became the nation of Russia. Had we done both there would be no new Cold War as is being perceived today.

Instead of seizing the opportunity for building a peaceful future, the United States did the following things:

1. We announced victory in the Cold War and preened ourselves on our success (which we continue to do today);
2. We sent some limited assistance to Russia in building institutions of democracy and free enterprise trumpeted as a "Grand Bargain", but pressed destructive "shock therapy" which caused GDP to fall no less than 37 percent, causing 3.4 million excess deaths 1990–1998.

3. We moved our Cold War military alliance, NATO, closer to Russia, thereby appearing to threaten it militarily; and
4. We opposed Russian efforts to restore parts of its historical influence as a great power.

As Russia, faced with these actions and American sponsored "color revolutions", took ever more hostile positions, we pressed forward trying to absorb more and more nations on Russia's periphery into the Greater Europe project. The Kremlin's annexation of Crimea was the predictable result. Instead of a secure peace, we now have an on-again off-again second Cold War.

Another very significant lost opportunity has been our failure to restrain the proliferation of nuclear armaments in the world.

Other lost opportunities include our failure to make a successful exit from our occupation of Iraq and our failure to be patient enough to encourage pro-democracy revolutions (so-called "color" revolutions) when they had an opportunity for success instead of encouraging them prematurely as we have done.

Significant as it is, this list is only a few of the multitude of opportunities which have been squandered by the United States during its few decades of world hegemony. It is a miserable record. It is no excuse to say that we were seeking good things, but that they were unattainable because there was opposition. Of course, there was going to be opposition. We failed to overcome it. The major failure was ours, no one else's.

It is hard to escape the conclusion that America has compiled this record of lost opportunities largely due to the incompetence and fecklessness of our recent presidents, each of whom has been a short term political-only thinker instead of a statesperson. It is not too much to say that these presidents may well have lost the future of the world — peace was attainable, and they failed to attain it. That they each claimed to be seeking peace is no excuse in the world of reality — what matters are results.

We had several years to help the Russian people and didn't do it right; the result is Putin.

We had several years to help the Afghan people, and didn't do it right; the result is chaos in Central Asia.

We had several years to help the Iraqi people and didn't do it right; the result is a failed nation under Iranian control and the emergence of ISIS.

Given this record there are things America should not do.

Specifically, America should not seek Sole Superpower Status (SSS) or the dominance or hegemony which potentially accompanies it. There is a temptation to try to return to the 1990s and the first decade of the 21st century when America had such status. The temptation arises because sole superpower status suggests that we could then deal with the challenges we face successfully — we could confine China within its borders; we could eliminate ISIS; we could de-nuclearize North Korea and Iran; we could confine Russia to the small-power role which is all we think her economic status entitles her to.

The problem with this aspiration is that we no longer have the resources and will to accomplish it. Regaining sole superpower status would require remilitarization on a large scale. It would also require more political consensus than we now possess. We are a deeply divided country which can no longer maintain a consensus-based policy and so we have to cut back what are likely Trump's aspirations. This is a realistic appraisal of American capability today.

Specifically, America should not accept subordination to other powers or to international institutions like the United Nations. Subordination dispossesses our people. It makes us the servants of others. We should not accept a role as part of the international mob.

- Politically accepting subordination is an error because it ties us to the aims of others rather than our own and imposes on us an unfair burden of responsibility for others' defense and objectives. We should withdraw from the webs of self-seeking and influence-peddling which are international organizations.
- Subordination is sometimes justified as a use of soft-power, but soft-power is a mirage. There is no such thing as soft power. Power comes from money and guns. As Mao said, "Power comes out of the barrel

of a gun." ("*Problems of War and Strategy*" November 6, 1938). Soft power is influence. It is not power. Influence is very valuable but it shouldn't be confused with power. Influence we can attain in the world without involvement in international organizations which result in America's subordination to the agenda of others.

Specifically, America should not over-reach in the multiple ways which we have been doing.

The United States is now placing small numbers of troops and advanced weapon systems in the eastern members of NATO which are countries which not long ago were elements or satellites of the Soviet Union. This is an error. The American weaponry and troops are not sufficient to defeat a Russian attack; they are only sufficient to trigger American involvement in a conflict in Eastern Europe should one break out. The presence of American troops and weapons in Eastern Europe does reassure our allies of America's commitment in case of conflict, but they do so at the cost of our own flexibility and independence. We are therefore over-reaching from the perspective of our own security when we make these gestures in Eastern Europe.

Furthermore, the United States is now confronting China and militant Islam as well as Russia militarily across the globe. These engagements constitute a very substantial challenge to American power. We are doing this without allies who can carry much weight, and both American political parties are supporting this likely over-reach. In the 2016 presidential election contest only Senator Rand Paul among all the presidential candidates of both parties expressed serious reservations about American over-reach. The weaker the United States gets — our military is suffering badly today from over-bureaucratization — the more belligerent and wider our outreach seems to become.

The Myth Of Collective Security

Following chapters will recite a litany of challenges to America in the world, all of which have the present reality or possibility of violence. Faced with an increasingly daunting world, American politicians scramble for cover. An effective dodge is the notion of allies — of coalitions which are assembled to help us meet danger. But collective security is very insecure.

Collective security has become an objective in itself. Challenged by Wolf Blitzer of CNN about Administration failures in the war on terror, a State Department spokesperson replied that the United States is working with an international coalition against terrorism and added that "this is an accomplishment itself." Thus, a supposed means to American security which is not working becomes an end in itself. This is consistent with the broad legalistic attitude now dominating so many American minds: that the process is a goal in itself quite independent of any result the process is supposed to accomplish.

Americans generally presume that coalitions are an effective way to deter or counter an opponent. This is often not the case. A coalition is an especially fragile way to attempt to wage war. Coalitions require continued effort to keep the alliance together politically; they are difficult to get to accept strong leadership from an individual and so tend to be directed by committees from the various powers, which is a very bad way to wage war — it tends to be indecisive and conflict-ridden. The forces which a coalition puts into the field have continuing and substantial problems of communications and supply because of the different languages and systems which are ordinarily in place in different nations' armies. Hence, coalition forces are very difficult to coordinate effectively. So difficult, in fact, are the problems of coalitions in actual battle that ordinarily a single unified power is far stronger than a coalition of similar size and forces, so that a coalition has to have significant force superiority. Finally, in many instances, a coalition is not really a combination of force at all — it is one nation's military supplemented by others in order to acquire bases or for political purposes. It is for all practical purposes of war, a single power. When Coalition forces invaded Iraq in the second Gulf War, the victory was won by American forces with appreciated but minor support from the other members of the Coalition.

There are some exceptions, and they are notable, if few. The British and the Germans combined to overthrow Napoleon at Waterloo. The

Americans and British combined to defeat Nazi Germany in France and the Low Countries. In these instances, the partners were of roughly equal weight in the coalition forces. When a coalition is one major power and many minor ones, then the major power is probably better off without the other coalition members, except, as stated above, to acquire bases.

In the world today, the United States has no allies of comparable power to our own. We therefore have no opportunity for effective military coalitions. We must fight our conflicts alone. Therefore, the United States military budget must be of a size adequate to defeat potential enemies. It can impose on allies a requirement to defend themselves only if the United States is prepared to see them defeated. America cannot rely on a coalition in which each party bears a proportionate share of the military burden. So a Western coalition in which each nation pays a certain percent of its GDP to maintain a military force will be a very weak military player on the world stage. What is possible is for the United States to require its allies to pay the United States for maintaining military to defend the entire coalition, so that the financial burden is shared equally.

Today's issue is not, therefore, whether or not the United States can get our NATO or SEATO allies to contribute a proportionate share of the military to a common defense — this is a sure recipe for defeat — but whether or not the United States can get our allies to bear a proportionate share of the financial cost of the common defense, which the United States will, and must, provide. So, we must continue to outspend the world in defense, and we must use the money well. We must also see if we can persuade or compel our allies to bear a reasonable share of the cost of the common defense. We cannot cut the United States defense budget and expect to rely instead on the military forces of other nations. If we do that, we are in actuality reducing our expectations of what can be defended for us in the world. It is a way of de-establishing the Pax Americana and commentators in other countries have already pointed this out.

Our allies are generally a military liability — we have to defend them and they bring almost nothing of military value to help us.

A classic example may be taken from World War II. When Hitler invaded the USSR his forces were accompanied by those of Italy, Rumania and Hungary. The Germans deployed the forces of their three allies to protect the northern flank of the German Sixth Army as it thrust toward Stalingrad. When the Russians sought to break the German grip on Stalingrad, they attacked the north-western flank of the German armies. The Italian, Rumanian and Hungarian forces collapsed virtually instantaneously (in part, it should be said in fairness, because they were not equipped with anti-tank weapons and were overrun by large numbers of Soviet tanks). It was the collapse of these allied forces that initiated the German disaster at Stalingrad. His allies brought Hitler nothing, and Hitler spent much needed resources to defend each of them from attacking Russian armies.

America's current coalitions so carefully and expensively assembled are of little or no military value and are primarily to provide political cover for the decisions of American presidents.

An Increasingly Pacificist Electorate And Allies

Jeremy Corbyn is the leader of Britain's main opposition party, the Labour Party. He has been in Parliament over three decades. He is adamantly anti- American. He views the United States as part of an imperialist world. He opposes war, including the American actions in Afghanistan and Iraq after the 9/11 attacks. It is not clear what he thinks the United States should have done in the aftermath of the attacks. Corbyn is an example of an attitude which is having great influence among our European allies. It is a basically pacifist attitude.

Polls in Europe show that many Europeans oppose their own countries, members of NATO, joining in the defense of another NATO member if it is attacked. "At least half of Germans, French and Italians say their country should not use military force to defend a NATO ally if attacked by Russia,' the Pew Research Center said it found in its survey, which is based on interviews in 10 nations," wrote Michael Gordon in *The New York Times* in June, 2015.

The defense effort made by our NATO allies is steadily declining. This is especially interesting in face of a rising threat from Russia. Military spending by NATO members has been steadily falling. Over the past decade military spending by NATO member countries has declined to less than two percent of GDP on average. In 2014 military spending by NATO members declined by 3.9 percent in inflation-adjusted terms. In 2015 military spending declined another 1.5 percent in inflation-adjusted terms. These declines were in the face of increased threats from Russia. The declines accompanied increasingly bellicose warnings from NATO to Russia.

The Russians are certainly watching NATO's actions, and not crediting NATO's rhetoric. So the position of the United States is that it leads a military coalition that is disarming while issuing threats. If a conflict emerges, the United States will be called upon to supply the military force to back up NATO threats, and it may find itself without effective allies.

This is a very bad situation for our policy to put our country into.

Collective Security As A Political Fig Leaf

Militarily, America's involvement in international organizations, including military alliances, is of little value to us except in gaining some bases overseas. With a few exceptions in some specific situations, the military contribution of America's allies is minimal. Collective defense has not worked in recent centuries — a dominant power has to bear almost all the burden and allies frequently collapse and are a source of vulnerability.

It serves very important domestic political purposes, however, for American politicians to be able to assert that we have allies in overseas engagements and are not operating on our own. First, it suggests that others believe in the correctness of our mission. Since the American electorate is so deeply divided on partisan and ideological lines at the moment, and whatever party is in power is distrusted by the other, a show of international support is useful in gaining domestic support for a policy.

Second, having other nations behind us suggests that we will obtain useful military support from them. It implies that we will bear a lesser burden in lives and expense.

Both points in favor of coalitions and allies are invalid. First, we generally obtain allies by the inducements we offer them, not because they support our missions. Second, allies rarely provide significant military assistance to us.

It does not hurt to have allies; it does not hurt to be supported by a coalition. But it is a fraud to suggest, as many American politicians do, that allies or a coalition will do our fighting for us, or even significantly reduce our load. For example, the Obama Administration sold the Iran Nuclear Agreement in part on the assertion that there was strength in collective security and multinationalism — that is, that it is significant that there is a group of powers involved, not just the United States. Yet, these same powers had failed to support fully the sanctions which should have made the nuclear agreement unnecessary. It is unlikely that if stringent methods should be needed to enforce the nuclear agreement, that these powers will engage in them. If the agreement is to be enforced, it will be the United States that must do it. Iran is, of course, fully aware of this, but it suits Iran's geo-political purposes at this point, as it suits those of the Western powers, to pretend that the nuclear agreement is effective and enforceable by a coalition.

It is even untrue to suggest that any of our current allies or coalition members will add much to our strength if we do most of the fighting. This is a clear lesson of history; it is also a consequence of our current situation. In general, the countries with whom we are ordinarily allied are both weak now and are further weakening themselves intentionally. With the exception of providing useful bases so that our forces can operate from nearer an enemy, we obtain little from our allies of military value. Instead, our allies generally require more support than they are worth.

In the Second World War we had dozens of allies. Except for bases only two provided significant assistance in defeating Germany — Russia and England — and none provided significant assistance in defeating Japan.

The same is true today. If we get into a war, we will have to win it ourselves.

Trump may propose that the United States should abandon collective security (following George Washington's and Thomas Jefferson's advice — to avoid entangling alliances). The United States is weakened in multiple ways by the alliances and would do better with greater independence of action.

Our security should be sufficient motivation for us without requiring the support of allies. We should not need other countries' ratification of our objectives and methods. Collective security shows not strength but insecurity — lack of confidence in our own motivations and strength.

The NATO Illusion

NATO is our most significant military alliance and it is most highly regarded by commentators. Its agenda sounds important. But today NATO is accompanied by steady cuts in the defense spending of almost all its members to quite low levels. The contribution of NATO members to the common defense of Europe is steadily decreasing and what contributions are made seem to lack readiness of forces.

NATO holds periodic conferences attended by the heads of state of the member nations. It adopts significant sounding resolutions and policies. In 2008, at a meeting in London, NATO defense ministers agreed to begin a debate on strengthening the Alliance's common defense and deterrence capacity. Two years later, in Lisbon, NATO adopted a new strategic concept which obliged its members to reinforce collective defense as the Alliance's first core task. Conclusions reached at the 2014 summit in Newport, Wales involved strengthening the NATO response forces by integrating force units, moving to very high readiness, and establishing a multination corps to command operations. The pre-war positioning of American troops and weapons on NATO's eastern front was agreed and the United States promised to move troops and weapon systems east to confront Russia.

All this sounds very significant, but NATO does not have forces in position to counter a Russian strike in Eastern Europe. If there were such a strike, a massive exertion of force by America would be required to defeat the Russians. Reliance by the American public on NATO is an illusion.

Despite all this, it is common for defense commentators to find reasons to praise NATO for its contribution to collective defense. For example, in an article entitled "*5 U.S. Weapons of War Russia Should Fear*" the author wrote, "While not a 'weapon' in the traditional sense, the U.S. global alliance network would greatly enhance America's ability to wage war against Russia. In this sense, it is telling that Russia lists NATO (rather than the United States) as its greatest security threat." The author apparently gives significant value to the military capabilities of our allies and discounts totally our allies ability to persuade us to intervene on their behalves, not our own. The article sites Russia's listing NATO, not the United States, as its greatest security threat as evidence of the importance of NATO.

It is not the military significance of NATO that concerns the Russians. It is its political significance as an instrument of German aggrandizement. Further, NATO suggests to the Russians that the United States, with its very significant military power, is backing Germany's ambitions in Eastern Europe. Russia is concerned about Germany. NATO is synonymous with Germany. The Russians until recently saw America controlling Germany; hence, NATO = Germany = America. The Kremlin's attitude is shifting because Germany is asserting its independence from the United States and is demonstrating its newly emerging hegemony over the European Union.

With this alternative interpretation in mind, it becomes clear that NATO is not an expression of Western strength, but is a dangerous involvement for the United States. Because of American participation in NATO, Germany is now in a position to involve us in conflict with Russia. Already, we have been drawn into diplomatic conflict with Russia which keeps us from working with Russia against Islamic terrorism and in constraining China. We might also be drawn into military conflict with Russia in Eastern Europe. Worse, any conflict with Russia could become nuclear in form.

Americans seem not to realize this danger despite its importance.

The New Anglo-Saxon Bloc

The coalition that joined the United States to wage the Cold War was composed of two groups — continental European nations and a world-wide grouping of Anglo-Saxon nations. For decades these two groups formed one body which the United States led. With the British vote to leave the EU, this coalition is fracturing. There is no current change in NATO, but there is a big change in the international political alignments which underlie NATO.

The British vote to leave the European Union has inadvertently recreated an Anglo-Saxon bloc in the world. The United States does not yet know what it will do as the necessary leader of the bloc, and the other member nations of the bloc, including Britain, do not yet have clear expectations what they will do within the bloc. But the remaining EU members, which now constitute a continental European bloc of the sort that we have seen often in history before, are certainly perceiving an Anglo-Saxon bloc to be reemerging.

This is an important challenge to the United States, and a great opportunity. Because of actions in which we had no significant role, we suddenly find ourselves as leader of a continental European military alliance (part of NATO) and of an Anglo-Saxon bloc (also part of NATO). In both these blocs there is strong domestic political opposition to American leadership. This may be largely posturing by local politicians. Neither of these blocs, and none of the countries included in them, are able to defend themselves successfully against a major foreign power (Russia, China or even, soon, Iran). In both blocs, military effort is declining. The consequence is that despite anti-American posturing abroad, there is no alternative for these countries but to try to continue to huddle under the American military umbrella.

Nonetheless, posturing or not, defense effort is declining not only among the continental European members of NATO but also among the Anglo-Saxon members of NATO. There is a worldwide growth of pacifist sentiment among America's military allies.

The United States therefore faces an increasingly complex structure of foreign alliances, and pressure to increase its defense spending to offset declines in defense spending among its allies. This is a difficult situation for us. Internationalist cosmopolitan policy is likely to join the parade of pacifism and reduce America's military effort while continuing, or even increasing, our commitments abroad. This will thrust the United States into a position of significant over-reach. In a few years there will be a very unfortunate result.

A sane policy would hurry to determine what an appropriate American response is in this position. We would either reduce our commitments abroad to levels that our military effort will justify, or we will relinquish domestic needs for an expanded military effort. But such a hard-headed assessment and decision is beyond the cosmopolitans. Instead, there is confusion and silence from the current American administration.

Part II

Today's Dangers

The United States today faces a daunting series of challenges in the world. Our next president will have to address each of them. We discuss the major ones in the next several chapters.

Chapter 8

Increasing Nuclear Risk

Doomsday Approaches

Probably the most disturbing aspect of the future Trump will face if elected president is that atomic weapons are now falling into the hands of people who will make a calculation about using them, and if they think the likely losses are tolerable, the weapons will be employed. The world is building toward a nuclear holocaust. The only question is when and where it will occur. Conflicts employing nuclear weapons are now likely within a few years. The *Bulletin of Atomic Scientists* already claims that the clock is only three minutes before midnight (the hour of doom)! According to the Bulletin, nuclear war is imminent.

Thus, it is probably not an exaggeration to say that the risk of nuclear holocaust is returning to, or today even surpasses, the risk level of the Cold War.

Though it did not seem so at the time, the collapse of the Soviet Union and the end of the Cold War provided a context in which the danger of nuclear war rose over the ensuing decades. The reason is significant. The initial response to the end of the Cold War was that war was less likely, and that therefore the use of nuclear weapons was less likely. What was not perceived was that the spread of nuclear weapons was more likely, and with it, the probability of their use.

The two superpowers who engaged one another in the Cold War had good reason to attempt to retain their de facto duopoly on the probable use of nuclear weapons. So although Britain, France, China and perhaps

Israel had nuclear weapons, the likelihood of their use was very low. Together the USSR and the United States were able to keep a lid on the possible use of nuclear weapons by third parties. Furthermore, the United States and the USSR had, during the Cold War, largely reached a modus vivendi with each other regarding the prevention of the use of nuclear weapons, although this was hardly failsafe.

After the collapse of the Soviet Union, it was generally presumed that the remaining superpower, the United States, could as effectively constrain the spread or use of nuclear weapons by other powers. This turned out to be incorrect. America seems to have failed completely to restrain the spread of nuclear weapons, despite very public efforts to do so over almost three decades.

Today it appears that the North Koreans have nuclear weapons; the Pakistanis and Indians possess them; the Japanese have a virtual capacity which can be activated in six months (according to Soviet intelligence sources); the Iranians have them now, or will in a few years; the Saudis may acquire them; the South Koreans are apparently considering acquiring nuclear weapons.

In all these cases, the nuclear weapons are strategic and a major limitation on their employment is a lack of long-range delivery systems. But those are being built.

Meanwhile, the Russians have been reactivating the Soviet strategic nuclear arsenal and upgrading its technologically, despite agreements to do the opposite. Also, the Russians are reactivating and improving the Soviet tactical nuclear arsenal and have publicly announced an intention to use tactical nuclear weapons in certain circumstances. This adds a significant new dimension to the threat of nuclear weapons being employed.

Nuclear War Is More Imminent Because Our Adversaries Are Better Able And More Willing To Endure It

During the Second World War, Russia (then the Soviet Union) and China both exhibited the willingness and ability to endure ruin and slaughter on the largest scale; and in its war with Iraq in the 1980s, Iran exhibited similar capacity. The West has never exhibited such capacity.

The result is that Russia, China and Iran, now the triumvirate of challengers to America, may well determine that they are able to sustain nuclear war successfully against the United States. If our challengers believe that the United States will respond to a nuclear attack only commensurately — that is, tit-for-tat — rather than with an all-out nuclear response, then a resort to nuclear weapons by our challengers is made much more likely. They may conclude that they can inflict on us, from their weaker military positions, nuclear attacks which we cannot bear and our retort to which they can themselves endure. That is, they will conclude that they can survive the limited nuclear response the United States will make, though they could not survive an unlimited response such as the United States has the capacity to deliver.

The conclusion our major adversaries may reach is that the United States will not use its full power, and so can be bested. The American policy of the past decade makes this conclusion virtually inescapable, and makes nuclear war much more likely than it was previously. Thus, it is not only proliferation that makes nuclear war more likely, it is the likely American response to a nuclear attack. Our probable response may seem limited and ineffective because of the willingness and ability of our rivals to endure nuclear attack. This makes nuclear war much more likely. US doctrine assumes the opposite. It insists that total destruction will be assured, and therefore that nuclear war is virtually impossible.

How Not To Be Concerned About The Risk Of Nuclear War

One way to not be concerned about nuclear proliferation and America's failure to constrain it effectively is to believe that no nation which possesses nuclear weapons will use them. This is an additional large step into the world of wishful thinking.

Another way to avoid being concerned about nuclear proliferation is to ignore the danger posed by nuclear weapons. Many Americans seem to have adopted this course. Considering the danger posed by the proliferation of nuclear weapons, it seems bizarre that so much more public attention is devoted to threats such as climate change.

Nuclear Protection For Vicious Regimes

The increasing risk of nuclear war provides more than enough concern for each of us. But nuclear proliferation not only threatens nuclear conflagration, it also protects vicious regimes from intervention by the United States or other powers on behalf of the regime's people. This is the major function of the atomic weaponry of North Korea; it is a key purpose of the effort of Iran to obtain nuclear weapons.

Given today's American public attitude about nuclear war — that any form or amount is not acceptable — then any nuclear weapons at all are a major advantage to authoritarian or rogue powers. This is because any nuclear weapons become a sufficient deterrent against intervention by the United States, no matter what the provocation.

Asia As A Nuclear Hotbed

It is likely that the most difficult area of nuclear proliferation to manage will be Asia, particularly the Far East and Indian subcontinent. India and Pakistan have long had nuclear weapons. But their contest is not a national contest but a religious one — Hindu versus Muslim. If Iran acquires nuclear weapons, and perhaps Saudi Arabia, it is possible that those weapons will be used to support Pakistan if a nuclear conflict arises between Pakistan and India.

Meanwhile, despite decades of bipartisan effort by the United States to deny nuclear weapons to North Korea, even Obama Administration supporters acknowledge that the rogue regime is making rapid progress. "North Korea could be on track to have an arsenal of 100 nuclear weapons by 2020," wrote the Editorial Board of *The New York Times*, "according to a new research report. The prediction, from experts on North Korea, goes well beyond past estimates and should force renewed attention on a threat that has been eclipsed by other crises."

North Korea's steady progress toward the capacity to deliver nuclear weapons against its foes demonstrates the failure of American policy with respect to North Korea. It also illustrates the failure of our broad non-proliferation policy. A less restrained, more violent policy against North Korean nuclear capability years ago might have succeeded in ending North Korea's nuclear threat. This is the sort of policy Israel proposed against Iran's nuclear program and that the United States rejected. The danger is that these chickens (peaceful, diplomatic efforts to limit nuclear proliferation) may soon come home to roost in rogue states armed with nuclear weapons and conflicts involving the employment of those weapons.

In the Far East, where North Korea and China now each possess nuclear weapons, a nuclear conflict becomes much more likely if the American nuclear deterrent directed on behalf of Japan and South Korea against China and North Korea becomes less credible. This is likely to happen if China and North Korea, individually or both, develop strategic delivery systems whose missiles can reach the continental United States. Will America sacrifice its West Coast cities to defend Japan and South Korea from China and/or North Korea? It is possible that Japan and South Korea may develop doubts and feel a necessity of arming themselves to deter Chinese or North Korean aggression.

American policy needs to be made for such eventualities. As Napoleon insisted, America will have to do a calculation of combinations and chances. We are calculating here combinations and chances based upon a realistic assessment of the aspirations of major nations and the changing constellation of power among them. Trump's calculations are likely to point toward an American policy that recognizes a rapid proliferation of nuclear weapons and the increasing likelihood that they will be employed. Other than deplore this situation or ignore it, we recognize no American policy response. If the Iran nuclear deal is offered as a policy response, we point to the many valid criticisms which suggest that it will be fruitless.

Unless the United States is prepared to destroy the nuclear weapons or delivery capability, or both, of nations now acquiring such capability (including North Korea, Iran, and possibly others), then there is no alternative but to plan for a world in which atomic war becomes likely. This will require the United States to withdraw substantially from regions in which it is likely to be drawn into nuclear conflicts. If one were to credit the Obama Administration with a policy-making capability directed at the interests of the United States, then perhaps its withdrawal from the Middle East is in recognition of the looming likelihood of a nuclear conflict between Sunni and Shia powers.

Today's Greatest Nuclear Threat

Although Asia presents the most complex arena of nuclear proliferation and consequent threat, the most immediate and severe threat is now Russia. Russia is the most fully armed and capable nuclear power. It is also the most opportunistic. It has developed and is steadily improving both strategic and tactical nuclear capability. While it adheres to the Soviet Union's strategic nuclear policy, and so is not likely to initiate a nuclear conflict, it is now advancing a much more aggressive tactical nuclear policy.

Russia has the most to gain by aggressive opportunism in world politics because it has the need to strengthen itself. It has already embarked on such courses in Ukraine and in Syria. It is expected to do so in the Baltic region. It carefully assesses the willingness of its potential opponents to actively intervene with force against its aggressions. It appears to assess the American willingness to thwart its actions as very low. Hence it is tempted to take steps that other powers, including China, Iran and North Korea, are currently deterred from. In consequence, Russia, not one of the nuclear proliferators, has emerged as the most dangerously aggressive member of the nuclear club.

For this reason, the incident in the late fall of 2015 when a Turkish jet shot down a Russia warplane over the Turkish-Syrian border is probably the closest the world has come to a nuclear conflict in decades. We do not know the details of the events by which the world avoided such a catastrophe. This is not unusual. In the case of the almost nuclear holocaust that was occasioned by NATO's Able Archer defense exercise in the 1980s, it was about twenty years before the details leaked out to the world.

The situation in 2015 was reminiscent of the outbreak of World War I. Turkey is a member of NATO; if attacked, the treaty requires the other NATO members to come to its aid. Yet Turkey acted against the Russians without prior consultation with NATO, as far as yet disclosed. The Russians might think that Turkey acted with full NATO consultation and approval. The Russian description of the Turkish attack as an intentional provocation suggests they may think that. If Russia had retaliated against Turkey, would a wider war have begun before American and European leadership was aware of the risk?

The matter was extremely dangerous. Putin had declared his willingness to employ nuclear tactical weapons. The Russians likely thought that Turkey was acting on behalf of NATO and so that it had to respond not just to Turkey but to NATO. If that had occurred, Russian nuclear weapons might have preceded Russian tank armies into Europe.

On the Western side, the situation was in the hands of civilian politicians. Article 5 of the NATO treaty does nothing more than obligate the parties to wring hands if one is attacked. This is generally misrepresented as a binding commitment of each member to defend another member if attacked. But how would the Western politicians have acted. Probably they would have left Turkey to its own devices against Russia. But they might have acted differently, desiring to appear resolute to their constituents and believing, probably erroneously, that Russia was weak and as ineffective militarily as it is economically. Something like this happened at the outset of both World War I and World War II. In 1914, at the outset of World War I, the British intervened against Germany on the basis of an agreement to defend Belgian neutrality which could have been interpreted quite differently (allowing Britain not to enter the war). In 1939, Britain intervened against Germany on the basis of a guarantee it had given Poland despite there being no treaty obligation.

In 2015 the Turks had seriously provoked Putin. He required quick placating or a devastating blow was likely to be delivered against Turkey and perhaps NATO. At that time, Russia's top defense analyst observed to a reporter "Nuclear War Over Turkey Shooting Down Russian Jet 'Likely.'" War was avoided. The Turks, responding to influences not yet made public, mollified Putin and a major conflict was avoided. Whether America played a constructive role in avoiding a nuclear disaster in this instance is unknown. Probably not. The American Administration has in recent decades seemed out of its depth generally in world politics; and in this situation it was likely at the bottom of the ocean.

In summary, the Turkish-Russian incident in the fall of 2015 offered a sudden and unexpected risk of a nuclear war and left the initiative regarding the war entirely in the hands of the Russian leader. Both represented major failings of American policy. The result is that we live each day with the potential for a sudden and unexpected outbreak of nuclear conflict. Furthermore, the frequency and risk of such incidents is rising as nuclear proliferation extends itself.

Chapter 9

Russia: A Drunk Soccer Hooligan?

Americans, by and large, do not respect Russia. A typical example is an article that appeared recently in *the Boston Globe*. It was entitled, "Putin's Russia is a Poor, Drunk Soccer Hooligan." Citing data about the Russian economy, the article sought to prove that Russia is a paper tiger.

However, Russia has the largest nuclear arsenal in the world (counting weapons with nuclear triggers temporarily removed). It also has the most powerful military, judged by its capacity to project power its neighborhood. This is especially important because Russia's neighborhood, unlike ours, includes the borderline of the confrontation of militant Islam with the West and also the confrontation of NATO with Russia itself. That is, Russia is currently able to project greater power in Eastern Europe against NATO than NATO can project in return. The view that Russia is a paper tiger ignores these things. Statistics about Russian living standards are irrelevant. The Russian people live relatively poorly, but that matters little to military strength. The United States seriously underestimates Russia because it mis-appraises Russia's economy. Yet the very fact of deprivation in Russia means that the Russian soldier is often much tougher than his Western counterpart. He does not need the massive support systems, including field kitchens, required by Western soldiers. In the American military, numerous people are required to support a soldier in the field. In the Russian military, the number is much smaller. Further, Russian soldiers endure much more suffering than do Western soldiers. In a nuclear war this could be of great importance. In all, the very economic weakness which Americans see as evidence of Russian military weakness is, to some large degree, a source of Russian military strength.

Western nations have often underestimated the Russians. Shortly before the Germans invaded the Soviet Union in June, 1941, Adolf Hitler told his generals about the USSR, "We have only to kick in the door and the whole rotten edifice will fall down." So the Germans kicked in the door of the Soviet Union. They kicked very hard. They invaded the USSR on a two thousand mile front with some three million soldiers and airmen. Four years later and after some four million Germans had died, the Russians overran Berlin and Hitler committed suicide. This was the most dramatic example of Western underestimation of Russia (it is not the only one — Napoleon had made a similar underestimate of Russian strength a century and a quarter before Hitler's error), and it points to a weakness in the Western assessment of potential Russian strength which continues to this day.

Russia lost more than territory and population with the collapse of the Soviet Union. It lost the ideological weapon of communism with its adherents all over the globe. Geo-politically what Russia lost was a fifth column in all Western countries. Communist adherents (the "party faithful") and sympathizers (so-called "fellow travelers") served the Soviet Union as spies, saboteurs, and political provocateurs.

Communist adherents were a powerful weapon for Russia. Replacing it may be cyberwarfare. Russia is likely the most aggressive country in hacking and cyber-spying. In a military conflict Russia might use its cyber capacity to disable enemies' power-grids, communication systems, and military command and control. These could have devastating impact on opponents such as the United States.

America is attempting to assess Russian capability in the cyber-world and to prepare protective counter-measures. But we will not have a reliable assessment of Russian capability until it is used against us. And this we hope to avoid.

Russia As A Military State

In the nuclear and cyber ages it is possible for Russia to have great military strength and modest economic strength. Russia is returning to its traditional role as a military state. Two decades ago we might have used our influence to affect that decision and mitigate it. If we had done so, today Russia would be on a different and less militaristic course. We failed to seize that opportunity, although our politicians pretended to be doing all they could to do so. As a result, today we have to decide whether or not we should oppose Russian geo-political ambitions or accept the Russians as a useful ally.

This sort of posturing while accomplishing nothing is characteristic of politicians in Western democracies. Angela Merkel commented, during her visit to the White House on February 9, 2015, "that is why we are politicians — because we believe in talking things out." She did not say, "that is why we are leaders — to go in the right direction." She did not say, "That is why we are politicians, to get things done — to accomplish what is possible." Instead, Germany's elected leader stressed talk.

By leadership most politicians in the Western democracies mean exhortation — "You people should do this or that." The difficult work is, of course, not the exhortation — words are cheap — but the doing. True leadership involves action, not merely talking things out or exhorting other people.

A Gaidar Institute report says that Russian "…military spending has doubled since 2010 and accelerated even faster since the Ukraine war. Defense now accounts for 35 % of government outlays, about 14% of gross domestic product." Though this estimate of Russian military spending may be overstated, perhaps the real proportion of GDP is about 8 percent, it should be obvious to any American reader that this level of military effort exceeds that of the United States (in which about 5% of GDP goes into military spending — even though the absolute level of American spending far exceeds that of the Russians).

Russian rearmament has a domestic, as well as a geo-political, purpose. A Kremlin military adviser told *Bloomberg News* in 2014 that "intensifying the development of the military industrial complex" would end Russia's "macroeconomic stagnation". That is, military rearmament would provide economic growth and improved employment levels. This is, of course, what increased military expenditures did for the German economy in the late 1930s and for the American economy in the 1940s.

Putin is quoted telling the Russian "defense industry leadership" at a meeting in Sochi in 2014 that "All questions relating to adequate resource allocation (to the Russian Military Industrial Complex) should have been resolved."

Russia's Endangerment And Its Defensive Aggressiveness

Russia deserves special attention from American leaders not only because it is potentially dangerous, but because it is in a very special situation. It alone of the great powers is in danger of dismemberment — that is, it alone is in mortal danger. Because of this, Russia is defensively aggressive and unpredictable.

Russia is vulnerable because its enormous natural resources and low population make it a target for its neighbors. It lives in a very rough neighborhood including China, North Korea, Japan, the Islamic world and eastern and central Europe. Of these, China is infiltrating Russia's Far East and Siberia; Islam eyes Russia's Muslim areas enviously; and the European Union is encroaching on Russia's western borders.

What preserves Russia today are three deterrents. China is deterred from aggression by Russian nuclear weapons. Fifty independently targetable nuclear warheads which Russia possesses mostly in the Far East are sufficient to deliver a blow to China that will be crippling. Russia has a great many times more warheads than does China. China is biding its time wisely.

Islam is deterred by Russia's conventional weaponry. At the moment no power in Islam is able to challenge Russia successfully. On the contrary, Russia has repressed its Muslim minorities when they have rebelled, and it has now entered directly into the Syrian civil war.

Finally, the European Union is deterred from incorporating more of the former Soviet Union into its military (NATO) and economic (the European Union) spheres by the full panoply of Russian power. This includes economic threats (Russia's hold on Europe's natural gas supply), Russian military action, as in Crimea and Ukraine, threatened military action against the Baltic States, and Russian political machinations.

Russia's direct challengers involve all the major powers of the world — China, Islam, and the European Union — except the United States. The United States, unlike China, the EU and militant Islam, has no territorial or other ambitions vis-à-vis Russia.

Russia's situation demonstrates that in today's world, as in the past, nothing but raw power restrains national ambitions. Russia survives because it is well-armed. A world order which supposedly rests on the maturity of nations as expressed in international law is here shown to be largely an illusion.

Because of Putin's revitalization of the Russian military, Russia is at this moment in no real danger from its neighbors. As long as Putin is in control, it is not likely to be. Russia is rearming quickly and reaching for supremacy in theaters of military operation like the Baltic states and Novorossiya, not just parity, over its rivals. Russia is due special consideration from American leaders for this reason also. It is again a significant challenger to the United States and one due to which, should we stumble into conflict, we would incur great risks.

The immediate danger to the United States is of involvement of America in a conflict growing out of the Russian situation. At the moment the danger is not of an attack by one or more of its neighbors on Russia — as we have seen above each of them is variously deterred — it is instead that Russia, seeking longer-term safety and restoration of former czarist Russian and Soviet sphere of influence, will reach to add territory, population and resources from its neighbors in Europe, the Middle East and Asia, the better to contain its rivals.

The Magnitude Of The Russian Threat To America

We expect that the next American President will be exposed to a Defense Department-like calculation of the magnitude of the threat to the United States from Russia and compare it to a similar calculation of the magnitude of the threat to the United States from ISIS.

The formula is simple arithmetic. The threat from a potential adversary is equal to the danger from that adversary times the probability of conflict with that adversary.

Threat = Danger × Probability

The notion embodied in the formula is that a danger may be very large, but if its probability of occurrence is small, then the threat it offers is much reduced.

The Threat from ISIS can be estimated as follows:

Danger: 3,000 Americans dead in a 9/11 type attack
Probability 80%
Threat (3,000 × 0.80) 2,400 dead Americans

The Threat from Russia can be estimated as follows:

Danger 100,000,000 Americans dead in nuclear exchange
Probability 1%
Threat (100 million × 0.01) 1,000,000 dead Americans

So the Russian threat to the United States is **416 times larger** than the threat to the United States from ISIS.

It is evident where thinking Americans should place their concern and concentrated attention.

Russian Conventional Military Capability

The Russian military threat is not confined to a nuclear exchange. We have noted previously that the West continually underestimates Russia's conventional military capability. Because there is now a growing concern in the West about the possibility of facing Russian troops, it is useful to review the evaluation of Russian military capability which was made after World War II. One of the best is included at pages 349–354 in a book entitled PANZER BATTLES, by German Major General F. W. von Mellenthin . Von Mellenthin spent two years (mid-1942 through mid-1944) on the Russian front and was engaged in the battles of Stalingrad, Kursk, and the defense of the Ukraine and Poland (each unsuccessful, of course). Von Mellenthin also served in the conquest of Poland in 1939, France in 1940 and the battles in North Africa in 1941–2, and in the defense of France in 1944 and Germany, 1945. Hence, he is able to compare Russian to Poles, French, British and American militaries from personal experience. His assessment probably has immediate validity today, for good and bad, if we were able to get the necessary information about today's Russian military.

Key Points From Von Mellenthin

1. Russians are very hardy soldiers
2. Russian command generally sacrifices the lives of soldiers without concern
3. Russians have an indifference to death of comrades and self in battle that makes them hard to stop
4. Russians have technical people who are very good
5. Russians have good equipment and employ it in large quantities
6. Russians are often inflexible in plans
7. Russians resist determinedly when attacked head-on; but
8. Russians are highly emotional soldiers — easily panic when surprised, but are sometimes determinedly persistent
9. Russians are very hierarchical — when command is missing, they are often immobilized
10. Russians are very good at combined force operations (infantry, mechanized units, and air power); not so good at naval operations.
11. Russian infantry are far less dependent on supply than Western armies; they live off the land and this is why scorched earth policies are necessary to slow their advance.
12. After long periods of peace, Russian leadership is often incompetent, but battle soon causes very competent leadership to emerge.

Americans have not seen the Russian military in large-scale operations since the 2008 invasion of Georgia (Gruzia). Western experts were not impressed, but Putin learned his lesson. Russia's combined arms warfighting capability improved dramatically thereafter including in Syria. Any criticism about the performance of the Russian military in Syria means little — it is the teething of a military. For example, in 1940 Russian forces were incompetent in an invasion of Finland. The Russian fiasco at that time helped persuade Hitler that the USSR could not successfully defend itself. But only a year later Soviet forces delivered a smashing defeat to the Germans before Moscow (a decisive battle little known in the West). A major difference between Finland in 1940 and Moscow in 1941 was that an extremely competent general had emerged to lead the Russians in 1941. Having Zhukov in command at Moscow made all the difference. The Russian soldier well-led is a formidable enemy. And the Russian high command, when it is experienced, is very good at tactics and strategy.

Russia At Risk

As we pointed out above, Russia is the only major power in danger of dismemberment. The danger is not from the United States. Russia has nothing to fear from the United States because it has no interest in Russian territory and because Russian nuclear capability is sufficient to deter any United States military aggression. In addition, the United States is largely unaware that others are interested in dismantling Russia. Putin is clear about the danger in his speeches to Russian audiences, but the United States ignores the message.

Russia is in danger from its neighbors. The threat is real because Russia, as it is constituted today, appears to lack the population and economic strength necessary to defend its vast and resource-rich territories which others covet. China and Islam are prepared to use force if an occasion arises against Russia in order to acquire population, territory and resources. The Germans, via the European Union and NATO, are adept at political aggression. It was a German effort to economically and politically bite off the Ukraine that led to Russia's recent seizure of the Crimea. The crucial importance of Crimea to Russia was made evident only a short time ago when Turkey shot down a Russian fighter and Russia began to assess its military capability against Turkey. Crimea is Russia's Black Sea base. Turkey is Russia's Black Sea adversary even though Erdoğan appears to be temporarily mending fences after surviving an abortive *coup d'etat* that some Turkish media are blaming on the United States. Without Crimea, Russia would be much weaker against Turkey.

Russia is currently able to deter Chinese aggression with Russia's nuclear weaponry. But over the next two decades — which is an appropriate time-frame for our national leaders to contemplate, though it seems much too long for most of our financial and political people to consider — there seem to be three things that could change the correlation of force between Russia and China and make Russia east of the Urals vulnerable to Chinese incursion.

1. A significant decline in the quality of Russian leadership (a new Gorbachev or Yeltsin);
2. Chinese advances in nuclear weaponry which allow it to impose an effective response to Russia's deterrent capability so that nuclear weapons are effectivity rendered unusable because their use would involve Russian national suicide); and
3. Chinese development of a strategic nuclear defense capability so that again Russia's nuclear weaponry is rendered unusable and so its deterrent is ineffective.

The Global Political Course Over The Next Two Decades — The Russian Opportunity

Despite the risks Russia faces from its neighbors, it also has a great global political opportunity over the next several decades. Putin seems to grasp this.

The opportunity arises out of the decay of the West and the collapse of the Western world order. It likely appears to the Kremlin that the West cannot succeed because of its continuing political and moral weakness and the contradiction in its fundamental value of multicul-turalism — the tolerance of intolerance when practiced by favored minorities.

Are the major rivals of the West in better position to succeed to the West's predominance in world affairs? Probably not, as perceived from the Kremlin.

Islam cannot prevail because of its fragmentation into Sunni and Shia and their animosity to one another.

Africa is not ready for world leadership.

China is not deeply interested in anything but natural resources and tribute from the rest of the world. It considers itself the center of the world and this limits its ambitions.

Russia is therefore in a unique position. It is unified, effectively-led, has clear ambitions without internal contradictions, and is strongly ambitious for expansion. If it can get its act together and plays its hand well, it can have a very successful run.

In this context, the United States is opposing Russian re-assertiveness but providing Russia an opportunity. This is another major inconsist-ency in our current approach which is causing unnecessary problems. Either the United States should oppose Russian revitalization effectively, or we should endorse it and benefit from it. What we are doing is enabling Russian expansion and alienating Russia at the same time. We thereby achieve the worst result possible — we help build a rival and embitter it against us. It is hard to imagine a more disastrous policy.

Three Alternatives

The United States has had three alternatives in approaching Russia.

Russia As A Friend

Americans, by and large, know little or nothing of Russian history and governance and have great difficulty putting themselves in Russia's position and therefore understanding why Russia does some of the things it does. The United States is protected by two great oceans, and it has as its neighbors Canada and Mexico, both peaceful states. The United States has no potentially aggressive neighbors. Russia is in a very different situation. It has aggressive neighbors all around it — some are aggressive militarily, some politically, some religiously. The United States feels safe; Russia feels endangered. Both are right.

The United States and Russia were allies briefly in World War I and were close allies for years in World War II. The World War II alliance fell apart in the Cold War and now most Americans seem to see Russia as an antagonist.

Perhaps it is fair to say that America and Russia are natural rivals — large nations with substantial national resources, proud histories, global reach and regional dominance. Rivals they may be; but historical experience says that they need not be antagonists. In fact, it is possible to argue that America and Russia should not be rivals at all. They are geographically separable. The United States and Russia have never fought a significant war against each other. If we continue to be fortunate, they never will. But the relationship seems doomed to being abrasive. This may be largely due to the United States. Russia and America have become rivals because America came after World War II to include Europe and Japan in its sphere of influence. Europe and Japan both border Russia and are major concerns for Russian leadership. Since the United States includes both Europe and Japan in its sphere of influence, the United States has become a natural rival for Russia.

In the aftermath of the collapse of the USSR, Russia suffered a devastating economic depression. The United States did little or nothing to mitigate this, and exacerbated it by giving toxic advice on "shock therapy". Instead, it offered to assist the Russians in setting up a stock exchange. The result was the death of some 3.4 million Russians from starvation and other consequences of deprivation. Later, when Germany via the EU sought to peel away Russia's former buffer states in Eastern Europe, the United States supported Germany. These events were directly responsible for Putin's revanche.

Putin's reaction is public record — he decided that America and the European Union were Russia's cynical adversaries and that realpolitik had to replace post-Soviet "partnership" with the West, protestations to the contrary notwithstanding.

Thus, the United States has already squandered its opportunity for friendship with Russia, even though the breach is not irreparable in the fullness of time.

Confronting Russia

American officials and advisors are generally agreed that Russia is now an enemy. "Matching Russia's multifaceted imperialism requires a multifaceted U.S. counterstrategy," wrote Robert D. Kaplan," the coordinated use of sufficient military aid, intelligence operations, electronic surveillance, economic sanctions, information and cyberwarfare, and legal steps." Note the reference to "Russia's multifaceted imperialism," and the call for martialling all of America's strength against Russia.

Further, the Defense Department is now pointing to Russia as America's "antagonist" and an "existential" threat to the United States because of its nuclear arsenal.

A less bellicose but equally antagonistic line is offered by the Carnegie Foundation for International Peace. The line is that Putin is merely an improviser. "The Ukraine crisis is even scarier than you think," wrote Andrew Weiss, vice president for studies at the Carnegie Endowment, on February 20, 2015. "Russia's strongman is making it up as he goes along". The suggested response is that confidence building can overcome "Kremlin fears and complexes" and so will save the day. That is, that even at this late date in our relationship with the successor state to the USSR, rhetorical American good will can placate the Kremlin and reduce tensions to friendship. This view is offered despite considerable detailed evidence from Russian military journals to the contrary. As is frequent in today's America, people who should know better inhabit an alternative universe of their own imagination, but find it useful as a domestic political tool.

The American Administration, in pursuit of its own version of the Carnegie suggestion, has implied that we are partnering with Russia in Syria to defeat ISIS. Only extensive evidence from Syria that the

Russians are acting to shore up Assad's regime with much higher priority than to defeat ISIS has forced the Administration to back off this pretense.

Both these approaches — one stressing American military strength as a response to Putin's Russia, the other stressing American appeasement — begin from the assumption that Russian geo-political objectives today must be countered — that Russia is an enemy until either constrained or converted.

Further, both these approaches make the assumption that the United States must act to restrain Russia's ambitions without any more fundamental assessment of America's own long-term interests or capabilities. It is not clear that we have the military capability to restrain Russia's ambitions; nor is it clear that to do so is entirely in our interest.

Because of Russia's exposure Russian action abroad is strategically defensive. In opposing Russian actions which are essentially defensive and mis-characterizing them as offensive, the United States is both perpetuating its Cold War mentality and denying itself a potentially valuable ally against China and militant Islam. The correct balance must be struck.

Russia As A Frenemy

Rivals or not, the United States and Russia have frequently been allies. We were allies in World War I and World War II, despite totalitarian governments in Russia in each war (the Czarist in World War I and Stalinist in World War II). The Cold War never became a hot war. We should not be enemies, but we cannot be friends. Hence, the proper concept of the American-Russian relationship is as frenemies.

It is hard to propose Russia as a frenemy in the middle of our current effort to include Russia among our enemies. Yet, today we share antagonists — militant Islam and China are the most important. Russia is better positioned to deal with both than is the United States.

Russia is already strongly ensconced militarily in the Middle East and President Obama has at times seemed willing to turn over to Russia dealing with radical Islamic terrorism. Russia may be better at it than we, but then we must concede the failure of the Western-oriented revolution in Syria. We must, therefore, concede some of our previous ambitions for the region. This may not be a bad result for America, however unfortunate it is for the Syrian people.

Russia is better positioned to deal with China than we are. Russia will fight. We are gradually being economically and militarily pushed out of the Far East.

Russia is now able to deter China via a few well-aimed nuclear weapons, and it has a great many. But as we have seen above, this could change. In a conventional war with the correlation of power which now exists, Russia will be no match for China. So if in the long-run the United States wishes to rely on Russia to help contain China, then Russia's conventional military potential has to be strengthened. So it may be Trump's best alternative to acquiesce in that.

The United States need not have Russia as an antagonist; we have no good reason to deny Putin's rebuilding Russian territory to some degree because a strong Russia is needed as a counter to China and Islam, and as a counter-weight to an increasingly assertive Germany.

A realistic and promising policy for the United States with regards to Russia is to cooperate frequently, maintain cordial relations, and accept that we are rivals and not close allies and never will be. This is a task not for military confrontation, but for effective and nuanced diplomacy. Putin can be satisfactorily engaged by an American Administration willing to accept a cold peace framework.

Because Russia is on the front-line of opposition to the ambitions of Islam and China, Russia is a natural ally of the United States in the Middle East and the Far East. Yet American politicians attack Russia with vigor continually. We seem returning to the extreme attitudes of the Cold War. This is likely a very serious error.

The Weak Get Beaten

In a memorable comment, Vladimir Putin observed about international relations, "the weak get beaten."

There are two ways to be weak: in strength or in resolve. At his point it appears that the major American weakness is in resolve; but a more physical weakness in strength is rapidly gaining ground.

Putin is currently operating like Stalin in the opening phase of the Cold War before the USSR was successfully contained by the West. He is moving opportunistically to advance Russia in many directions.

In this context, the West is hoping that Putin is a closet Gorbachev and therefore that the West can continue doing business as usual with Russia as it did in 1991. This means that the United States will be able to disregard defense and concentrate on social programs, even though the Kremlin is rapidly improving its armed forces. Russian actions repeatedly throw this wishful thinking into doubt. What is required now of the United States is a decision about what tack to take with Russia, as described previously in this book.

Chapter 10

The United States And Militant Islam

There is a significant political controversy in the United States about the nature of the terrorist threat. The Administration refuses to refer to it as "radical Islam," insisting that Islam is not the source of terrorism. Others insist that the threat is from radical Islam and that to deny this is to cripple our attempts to defend ourselves.

The controversy is off the point. In fact, the West, including the United States, is being challenged in many venues by Islam. It is being challenged spiritually, politically and militarily. The military challenge which we confront is limited at this point to terrorism because the military strength of the West so far overshadows that of any Islamic state or combination of states that Islam makes no military move. But, south of the Sahara Islamic para-military groups are active at a significant level. Should the military strength of Islam increase and that of the West decline, a military challenge from Islam is likely. The first place such a challenge might occur is Israel. This is the immediate danger of an Iranian nuclear weapon — that it will be used against Israel.

The challenge is from militant Islam, not simply from radical Islam. Terrorism is merely a tactic. If we could succeed in squashing terrorism, the other tactics (political and religious and even, perhaps, military) would continue. Perhaps Americans don't mind the challenge from Islam so long as it doesn't involve terrorism or direct military challenge. Perhaps we don't mind the challenge so long as people aren't dying. But this is to say that we are unwilling to defend our way of life, since Islam offers a direct challenge to it.

Terrorism is a tactic of the weak. Those who lack organized military capability or are reluctant to use it, resort to terrorism. Terrorism is today the weapon of choice of militant Islam. Those who engage in it are the radical elements of Islam, but they engage in it for the advantage of all Islam.

This is recognized in Islam generally. Hence, there is support for radical Islam throughout the Muslim world. Some Muslims regret terrorism because of its victims, but their regret rarely extends to disapproval and even more rarely to opposition to the radicals. Polls show clearly that all over the world Islamic populations are broadly supportive of efforts to expand the reach of Islam, including those made using the tactic of terrorism.

The spiritual challenge of Islam is to both Christianity and secular humanism (the new atheism which is advancing rapidly in the West).

The political challenge is offered in Western countries by Muslim immigrants and refugees who join with political parties already active. At this point, Muslims are minorities in all Western countries and participate in politics as minorities. The military challenge currently takes the form of terrorism, as we have said, or, in Africa immediately south of the Sahara, it takes the form of lightly armed quasi-military action.

It appears that some political parties in Western countries, specifically the Democratic Party in the United States, in appealing for Muslim support in domestic elections, are unwilling to attack Islam even to the terrorist challenge. Insiders in the American government are not concerned about conflict with Islam. Instead, they are interested in ingratiating themselves with Islamic governments for insider benefit. They are even more unwilling to accept that there is a challenge from Islam generally to the West.

Such a challenge exists. It has now been in process for more than fourteen hundred years. In that period Islam has waxed and waned. At one point it controlled most of India, and the entire Balkans in Europe. At one point Islam (in the form of the Turkish Empire) besieged Vienna. Now Islam is moving into Europe and America in two ways: peacefully via immigration and violently via terrorist attacks. As pointed out before, Islam's progress into sub-Sahara Africa is by military means that go far beyond terrorism (although they also include terrorism). What is now lacking everywhere, because Islam currently lacks the strength, is a major offensive military campaign launched by an Islamic nation state. At this point Iran and ISIS are the two competitors for that role — the first is Shia, the second is Sunni. Both major sects of Islam are thereby represented.

It is unfortunate that Islam is so aggressive. The West would prefer to avoid a conflict in all of the dimensions in which it is now being waged by Islam — spiritual, political and military. But a preference does not create a reality. To insist that it does, as the American government has been doing for decades, is to try to live in an alternative universe of one's own dreaming, rather than to accept the clear evidence that is before us.

Dynamics Of Today's Islamic Expansion

Islam is an ambitious religion. In a period when religion generally is in disrepute with the elites in the West, it is hard for most Americans and Europeans to acknowledge the grip which religion can have on its adherents. Islam has a strong grip on many people. It is now moving beyond its recent boundaries as Christianity did in the sixteenth through nineteenth centuries and as Islam itself did several times during its fourteen century existence. The expansion of Islam is into Africa and Europe and to a surprising degree into the United States (not elsewhere into the Americas and not into the Far East, but it already has a significant presence in the United States).

There is a dynamic process to Islam's expansion. It can be briefly described as follows.

- A few early arrivers and missionaries for Islam arrive in a host country, and achieve a foothold. They may be seeking sanctuary from the chaos they have left behind, desiring better economic opportunities, or the benefits of welfare in the West.

Thereafter, the early arrivers are followed by

- Immigrants, including refugees, who expand the foothold.
  Thereafter, militant groups within Islam follow to press their attitudes on the Muslim population which is already there and to press the host country to accept radical Islam both in the home countries of Islam in the Middle East and in enclaves in the host country. A key tactic is terrorism.
- Terrorists become active in the host country.
  Thereafter, if the host country is weakly enough organized and defended, well-organized lightly armed quasi-military forces arrive and terrorism rises to new heights and conquest begins (this is what is happening now in Africa south of the Sahara).
- Quasi-military forces lightly armed arrive.
  Thereafter, if the quasi-military forces are successful, fully organized main-scale military forces will arrive from Islamic countries for the purpose of conquest, occupation and control (this stage has not yet been experienced in our time).
- Full-scale, heavily armed military forces arrive.
  By the end of this process, all stages are likely operating simultaneously in the host (target) country. That is, while heavily armed military forces are conquering the region, immigrants are still arriving.

This is the process which Europe and the United States should now expect to experience. It is likely to take a long-time to mature, because at this moment both Europe and the United States are so well organized and armed that nothing of a military nature beyond terrorism is available to Islamic militants. ISIS is the cutting edge of militant Islam at the moment, and the most direct concern to the West.

ISIS

The Khmer Rouge are reputed to have had a saying:

To keep you is no benefit;
To kill you is no loss.

ISIS appears to have adopted a perspective similar to that of the Khmer Rouge. In response, it appears now that Western governments are unable to protect their citizens. French police knew Charlie Hebdo was a target, it had been fire-bombed before; the French police had placed security personnel at the Charlie Hebdo office; and yet the terrorist attack was fully successful. The Pulse nightclub in Orlando, Florida, had been visited by the killer several times before, and he had posted on social media his support for ISIS and his intent to take action; he was known to the FBI who had interviewed him several times; and yet the American federal authorities did not detain or arrest the killer before the attack. The World Trade Center had been bombed before; yet the American authorities were unable to prevent a second fully successful attack which took place on September 11, 2001.

Instead, after people have been killed, Western politicians give eloquent tributes to the dead and threaten retaliation against the terrorists. They take inadequate steps to prevent another occurrence — rather like shutting the barn door after the horses have fled. They investigate the attack and try to show that it wasn't terrorism, or if it was, that it could have been foiled by restrictions on gun ownership or some similar regulation. Then they go back to their ceremonial enjoyments until it happens again. Angela Merkel and François Holland tell the grieved to grin and bear the new normal because everything will be fine in the fullness of time.

What lies behind this behavior is an attitude. The attitude is driven by a calculation. The United States is a big country. It has some 319 million people. France is much smaller, but still has some 60 million people. Terrorists thus far have the means to kill only a few. The political calculation is that each Western country can endure the loss of a few hundred or a few thousand people; to accept this loss seems better than to disrupt political calculations that depend on Muslim support. Therefore, the death of a relatively few citizens is anticipated and the indignation that accompanies a terrorist attack is largely feigned. The politicians will deny such a calculation, of course, but it seems clear that it is made and its implications are accepted. This is the attitude that lies behind suggestions from political leaders that Western democracies must "learn to live with terrorism."

Hence, it is most likely that the danger to Western populations will grow. Efforts by Western police will falter against the political calculations of the civilian politicians. As our rivals gain strength they will support increasing terrorism against America overtly, as in the case of ISIS, or covertly, as in the case of Iran.

America's Iran Gamble

Although Islamic State is now the more visible enemy, Iran is the more important. Iran is a substantial nation state with a record of increasing importance in its region. The Obama Administration has seemed willing to cede dominance in the Middle East to Iran in various forms. The Administration seems to have judged Iran to be the rising power in the region, and does not wish to challenge it, but rather to cooperate with it. Since Obama seems to have an Islamophilic concept of American interest, this is consistent with his perspective. It may work. It is a gamble because we cannot be sure that Iranian ambitions will stop at the Middle East.

The Iranian nuclear agreement — whatever its own merits and whatever the motivations that led to American acceptance — is the Obama Administration's clear schizophrenic acceptance of a multipolar world in which the United States no longer wishes to try to impose its will or protect its allies, even though it never ceases trying. Obama Administration shadow spokespersons defended the Iranian Nuclear agreement on the grounds that the sanctions against Iran could not be expanded or extended to compel Iran to a different result because the Chinese and Russians, and some of the Europeans, would not go along. The Nuclear Agreement is said to be all that can be got out of the multi-power context. When Republican candidates said that the United States should apply more sanctions to get a better deal, the Administration replied, by implication more than directly, "You are living in the past. We no longer have the power to do that."

This is the first of the key lessons of this agreement: that the United States now accepts a fully multi-polar world when its presidents find it convenient to do so. We are no longer the world's sole superpower. We are one of several great powers (the Administration's shadow spokespersons even used the terminology, "great powers").

The second lesson is further confirmation that a multi-polar world is a world of nuclear proliferation. The Iranians are engaged in trying to proliferate. The Chinese seem unconcerned about proliferation, and the Russians follow their lead.

Probably Iran cares more about being able to import weapons and sell oil — which are now permitted because of the end of sanctions against Iran — while continuing to fund and promote the destabilization of the entire region, than about acquiring nuclear weapons. Iran probably maneuvered the United States effectively knowing that we were more concerned about its nuclear ambitions than in foiling its more significant objectives. Iran probably used the nuclear issue to gain what they desired more strongly. But it is also possible that Iran gained all it could have desired — an end of sanctions and the opportunity to acquire nuclear weapons.

Why The Iran Nuclear Deal Passed In The United States

There is a principle that what is important often cannot be demonstrated because it is well-concealed, but that what is important can often be correctly surmised. We suggest that Wall Street and European business interests were behind the Iranian nuclear deal. In other words, its primary motivation was not about nuclear weaponry, but instead the ending of economic sanctions. This is so even though the impact of Western financial and business interests on the deal was merely partial. The American Administration profited from the deal additionally by posturing as an agent of peace.

The situation is reminiscent of China in the early 2000s. There was every reason to proceed cautiously, especially with respect to admitting

China to the World Trade Organization, but the Bush Administration pushed forward without a safety net, because China was seen as a colossal commercial opportunity.

The Iranian government agreed to an international pact about nuclear weapons expecting to benefit twice: once when they signed it and once when they violate it. They have already profited from signing it; now they will look for the best opportunity to profit from violating it.

Why, however, did the American Congress accept the Iranian nuclear deal over the objections of the Israeli prime minister? How could this have happened given the supposedly strong influence of the American Jewish community on American policy-making.

A convincing clue appeared only a few months after the failure of objections to the nuclear deal in the American Congress. The November, 2015, issue of *Commentary* published a lengthy symposium entitled "The Jewish Future." All contributors were Jewish; all were American. Almost all contributors mention Israel. Only one of the fifty raises any doubts about Israel's successful existence in fifty years. Except that one exceptional contributor, none seems to take seriously an Iranian threat to Israel. The Israeli prime minister insists that the deal poses an existential threat to Israel, but the leading American Jews don't believe it. If this is the case, no wonder the Administration obtained acceptance from Congress of the Iranian nuclear deal.

Russia And Iran

In April, 2015, Russia lifted its ban on sales of S-300 missiles to Iran setting the legal groundwork for the possible Russian sale of a powerful air-defense system to Tehran.

What was Russia's motivation?

Russia began building Iran's nuclear capability in 1992. Although Russia has historically clashed with Iran over the Caspian Sea, it has cultivated Iran as an ally since the 1970s.

These initiatives appear to have been guided by Russia's doctrine of strategic opportunism. The Kremlin doesn't have a fixed end game, but tries to create conditions for windfall gains.

The missile deal may have multiple rationales including embarrassing the United States and the Saudis, and co-opting Iran into being an important Kremlin ally in dividing the Middle East.

It is not possible for us to be certain of Russian motivation. But whatever motive we choose to believe, we can be sure that the gesture isn't inadvertent.

Israel

For the moment, the Middle Eastern situation is developing in a way that seems advantageous to Israel. There are emerging three contending centers of power (Iran, Saudi Arabia and Egypt) and a group of failed (Libya, Iraq, Syria, Lebanon) or pacific (Morocco, Algeria) states. This increased fragmentation of the Islamic world allows Israel to engage in and change alliances with the contending forces, and thereby preserve itself. This is what the Crusader states in Palestine did before Saladin united the Arabs and pursued the destruction of the Christian states in the twelfth century. With no uniting force evident in the Middle East at this time, the strategic situation for Israel is improving, even as the West becomes increasingly feckless in its relations with Israel. The currently increasing strategic danger, of course, is the risk of Iran getting a nuclear weapon.

Failing In National Defense Policy

As we address the challenge presented by militant Islam we need to recall for how long our country has addressed but failed to surmount this challenge. Almost 50 years ago our business and political leaders were being warned in the Middle East against growing radicalism in the region.

According to David Rockefeller in 1969 President Gamal Abdel Nasser of Egypt told Rockefeller, then president of Chase Bank, that he was worried about the "growing radicalism and instability in the region."

It is now 46 years later and we have been unable to respond successfully to the challenge. It is much worse now, despite our having declared war on terrorism some fifteen years ago after the 9/11 attack on the World Trade Center. This record must be assessed as a significant failure of American policy and one that calls into question our entire approach to challenges not only from the Middle East but from abroad as a whole.

Islamic Extension

Here is a prescription from Ghassan Michel Rubelz, former secretary for the Middle East of the World Council of Churches, for countering Islamic militantism. He tells us that the favored American response to the Islamic challenge involves the following things — from both conservative and liberal perspectives. Integrate Muslim immigrants into European society, provide jobs, develop Middle East and North African economically, end deprivation, joblessness and alienation of Muslim immigrants Rubelz wrote, "Muslims…would add richness to Western societies and act as mediators of democracy to their countries of origin."

The problems with this prescription are that

(1) evidence is strong that most Muslims do not want to be integrated into Western society, resist it and try to transform their host;
(2) even if successful, integration will take a long time and will not immediately impact the warfare (or terrorism) occurring in Africa and the Middle East. So the prescription is not likely to work and even if it were to work, it is not quick enough.

Parallel emotionally and politically, if not logically, to the doctrine of defeat of militarism via domestic integration of Muslims into Western societies is a doctrine that has taken root in the West that insurgencies are defeated by winning the hearts and minds of civilians in the war-torn countries. There is very little evidence for this proposition. The defeat of the Communist insurgents in Malaya in the 1950s is often cited. But the victory of the British over the insurgents was largely due to the British interning the rural Malay population in armed camps so that the insurgents could be isolated and destroyed militarily.

Nonetheless, the United States pursues the doctrine of domestic "melting pot" integration as much as can be done in the context of brutal war. For example, in the Afghan conflict the American military announced that when Marines enter villages as part of the offensive operations, our Marines seek out opportunities to visit with the village elders to explain to them why the Marines are there. On the surface there is nothing wrong with this, but to believe that having Marines visit tribal elders will significantly advance the counter-insurgency is another example of wishful thinking, willful ignorance and pandering to various interest groups. A more than decade-long conflict suggests its futility.

There is embodied in the American approach to winning hearts and minds a fundamental contradiction that virtually ensures the failure of the American effort. The problem is best understood through an example. About twenty-two hundred years ago, Alexander the Great conquered what is now Afghanistan. In the process, he adopted local dress and customs. Plutarch, reporting Alexander's method, observed, "nothing gains more upon men than a conformity to their fashions and customs. "Yet, we Americans do the opposite. We bring our popular culture and our values — very different from those of Afghan Muslims — and we champion different fashions and customs at the very time we are trying to ally them with us. We do not adopt their fashions and customs in order to ally them with us; we do the opposite. It does not work.

In Afghanistan, the Americans pressured the Karzai government to reduce corruption and to advance the education of girls. Both moves had two purposes: one, to gain political approval in the United States and Europe, and two, to win the hearts and minds of the Afghan population.

The first was successful; the second not so clearly so. The second appears to have been based on a serious underestimate of the strength of Islamic culture and the reasons for its persistence. This was an expression of willful ignorance by the American leadership in Washington. Still, in much of the Islamic world, the traditional Muslim culture is eroding under the influence of European and American secularism and media, so that in the long run, if there is a long-run with American involvement, something like a change in Islamic culture is possible. But for that to occur would require a much longer presence of American forces in Afghanistan than was ever likely feasible in the American domestic political context.

Winning hearts and minds is not working.

There is an alternative approach. "He is master in Asia who seizes the people piteously by the throat," said Mikhail Skobelev, the Russian conqueror of Central Asia in the mid-nineteenth century.

The Chinese and the Iranians do this, and they are masters in Asia. We do the opposite and we are losing.

But it is not possible to conceive an American policy in Asia that is as ruthless as that followed by our authoritarian rivals; the American domestic political scene would not allow it short of a full-scale war of the type waged by America during World War II, when America accepts attacks on enemy civilian populations. For example, the subjection of a few Islamic terrorists to light forms of torture to obtain information in the immediate aftermath of the 9/11 attack resulted in a decades' long political imbroglio in the United States. If harsh policy is necessary to defeat insurgencies in Asia, then America is unable to succeed in anti-insurgency efforts and should not engage in them.

Measured Military Response And Bad Results

Closely akin to winning hearts and minds is the doctrine of measured military response. The American military now responds to hostile action with what is called "disciplined strength." If we are attacked, we respond with force commensurate with that applied against us. Size of units involved; the weapons employed; the geographic areas subjected to conflict — each is measured and responded in like. This seems a sensible thing. If someone strikes me, I should strike him back; not shoot him to death. Hence, this doctrine, like winning hearts and minds, readily obtains public support in the Western democracies. It is said to be an adult attitude.

The approach urged on us by American military leaders has always been the opposite of measured response. It is that if military action is taken, it should be taken with overwhelming force, so that the conflict is short and victory is certain. If warfare is short and victory achieved, then American and enemy losses will be minimized.

The problem is that measured response or disciplined strength means that the enemy will have time to learn better tactics and to build its own capability, so that American losses will always be greater than they need have been. In addition, the enemy will never be eliminated, but will always survive to continue the fight against us. This is precisely what has been occurring in our recent wars — in Korea, Vietnam, Iraq and Afghanistan.

We are not succeeding because our tactics, adopted to satisfy a domestic political audience, are ineffective. But like the classic definition of a fool, we continue to apply the same methods expecting a different result.

With clear objectivity we recognize that we cannot defeat Islamic radicalism by winning hearts and minds. We may be able to defeat it by force, but kindness will not work. Nor does measured response contribute to our success.

Finally, the mentality of the Near East is too complex for Americans to understand. When we say that others want the same things we do, that is too simple and not sufficient.

ISIS is a difficult problem for us if it is to be addressed with moderation and by winning hearts and minds. ISIS appears to have the right formula for success: a combination of terror and benevolence. The formula is terror to your enemies and benevolence to those who support you. This is the formula that put Lenin and Hitler and Mao in power.

It is America's good fortune that the great rift in Islam threatens the ultimate success of any Islamic movement. Thus ISIS is Sunni: Iran is Shia, and a unified Islamic state, or caliphate, is nowhere to be seen. Divided, it is difficult for Islam to conquer.

A broad conviction in Arab world is that the United States created ISIS by passing on weapons to them via the Iraqi forces. ISIS weaponry is American, not Russian, Chinese or Iranian. A further conviction is that the Americans now disguise their creation of ISIS by airstrikes against it. In the Middle East, evidence of America's support for ISIS is quickly cited. For example, Jordan degraded ISIS's military by 20% in 2 weeks; the United States hasn't done so in months. Why, because as bizarre as the supposition seems in America, the argument is that the United States supports ISIS.

A conviction that America first created ISIS and then tried to disguise its action by bombing ISIS involves more duplicity than Americans are comfortable believing exists, but this level of duplicity is easily acceptable to a Middle Eastern mentality.

Muslims engage in what they call cultural jihad aimed at Western society. Their allies are Western progressives embarked on a similar mission directed against traditional Western culture, but with a different desired result. This is why progressivism's supporters support militant Islam and refuse to acknowledge terrorism's Islamic connections.

Muslims believe that the United States is attacking Islam; and also that United States has created ISIS. These two convictions are inconsistent, of course. But they represent a Middle Eastern political constellation that is more complex than Americans are accustomed to or are adept at countering.

Chapter 11

Our Rivalry With China

China is a rival to the United States mainly because of the American presence in the Far East. China now aspires to a zone of special influence in the same area. The United States opposes this, and so there is the potential for conflict, intended or accidental, between the two great powers.

United States officials understand this thoroughly. The position articulated by senior American officials is that China benefits greatly from the American presence in the region and should not be trying to alter what has been the situation from the end of World War II until recently. During that time, the Americans insist, the United States has maintained peace in the region. Peace has allowed Japan, South Korea, Taiwan and most of all, China, to expand and modernize their economies without the burden of heavy defense spending and the destruction caused by war. Until the American peace, East Asia was continually at war and economic development was limited — in China, it was virtually halted for centuries.

The Chinese response is essentially that regardless of the merits of this American claim, the American presence is no longer needed. China — and that's all the Chinese care about — can now take care of itself — it needs no American protection.

Perhaps the most cogent explanation of Chinese thinking is this one, which was offered by a Chinese official to one of the authors of this book. "America has, in the Americas, its own special influence. No power from outside the Americas is allowed by the United States to establish significant influence or acquire territory in North or South America. This has been true for two hundred years. We, in China, think this is fine. It is appropriate for America to have such special influence in its own hemisphere. We in China simply seek the same type of influence in our hemisphere."

During the period of China's dominance in the Far East, about five centuries ago, "It became a confirmed Chinese attitude," wrote Colin Mason in his history of Asia, "that control of neighboring states was a prerequisite to the security of China." That is apparently again the Chinese attitude.

The core of the animosity between China and the United States today is that America is preventing China from reasserting control of neighboring states.

Secondary to the rivalry in the Far East is China's global ambition. For several years, China has been developing the military capabilities to protect its interests beyond East Asia. This is a very important development. China aspires to project military power in more and more of the globe. Certainly the Middle East (China's source of oil) and Africa (China's source of many raw materials) are included in the Chinese sphere of interest.

America faces difficult decisions with respect to three aspects of China's military development:

- First, China's development of long-range ballistic missiles that can hit the United States.
- Second, China's assertion of military control of the South China Sea.
- Third, China's development of global conventional military deployment capability.

Does the United States view with equanimity a Chinese expeditionary force in central Africa or in Iraq? These questions are now coming to the fore.

Current American policy, internationalist cosmopolitanism, is not likely to dissuade China from any of these three developments It is not likely to even address seriously Chinese nuclear capability and

Chinese global expeditionary ability. It is very disturbing that this is the case — it makes American policy seem obtuse for it fails to deal with real and growing challenges. A sane American policy would adopt a response to each of these three challenges from China and pursue their accomplishment vigorously.

Note that what is obtuse about American cosmopolitanism is not the course it adopts, but that it adopts no coherent course at all. What is sane about the alternative course we are examining is that it objectively assesses the challenges we face and adopts a coherent course in response.

Underneath the geopolitical reality lie intense commercial rivalries between America and China in the Far East. There may also be oil and gas fields under the seas that border Asia on the east which China is trying to take for itself from the nations of South-East Asia. Finally, China imports most of its oil and some other key raw materials through the Indian Ocean, the Straits of Malacca, around Vietnam and through the South China Sea to Chinese ports. At this point, the American military presence in the Far East means that the United States can interrupt that traffic at any point. China is concerned about the national defense implications of this, and so wants the United States military presence out of the region.

There is also a suspicion, well-grounded in history, that Chinese authorities, if faced by an economic down-turn and rising popular discontent, will seek to fuel nationalist enthusiasm via a foreign conflict. The United States would serve Chinese authorities well as a target of national aversion.

Thus, for economic and internal political reasons, as well as geopolitical ambitions, China and the United States are increasingly rivals. This rivalry has now progressed to the point of an arms race in the Far East. America is strengthening its military position in the region. "Rising defense budgets have fueled a sizable naval buildup in Southeast Asia," reports Richard A. Bitzinger, an analyst of the military buildup in Southeast Asia. "As a result, countries surrounding the South China Sea have acquired new military capabilities that could make conflict in the region, should it occur, potentially more lethal."

The United States is an enabler and a participant in this arms race. As an enabler we are helping our erstwhile allies fund their naval build-ups and we are providing weaponry to them. As a participant, we are building our naval forces in the region. President Obama has spoken of a pivot in American policy from the Middle East to the Far East — from Islam as the focus of American military interest to China. America is introducing a new class of warships (the littorals) designed to operate in the shallow, island-dotted waters of the South China Sea. China is now building submarines, developing new anti-ship missiles, and launching air-craft carriers in the South China Sea. America is using spy-planes and spy-satellites to try to peer into China's submarine pens on Hainan Island and to observe China's construction of artificial islands for military bases in the South China Sea. China is steadily increasing its military budget with annual defense spending growing at double digit rates. America is allocating more priority in its budget to weaponry and manpower with which to confront China.

Perhaps most provocative are Chinese largely man-made islands in the southern seas which lie in waters which are international or claimed by neighboring countries. These islands are being fortified by China. A key island (hardly even an island before the Chinese expanded it) is about 150 miles from the Philippines main island of Luzon, but some 550 miles from the nearest point in China.

These island military bases are like knives at the throats of Japan, South Korea, and Taiwan. The bases have the potential to cut their sea lanes from the Middle East and Europe. The bases are also of great potential value to China in a military conflict with the American navy.

In all this there is clear potential for conflict. But over the past several decades Americans have found reason after reason for being certain that there is very little chance of conflict with China. Often, these reasons have contradicted one another.

We should remind ourselves how quickly the general American attitude about China changes. In World War II China was an ally whose significance we exaggerated. We placed China on the United Nations Security Council treating it as a great power (presumably as a counter-weight to Japan, whose dominance in the Far East we were then in the process of destroying by military force).

After the war, a civil war emerged between the Chinese Nationalist government and the Chinese Communists. At the end of the war, a large section of northern China was occupied by Soviet Russian troops, and they had just destroyed in two weeks an army of a million Japanese in Manchuria, a large Chinese province. Soviet troops provided enormous material and moral support for the Chinese Communists.

There was much leftist support in the United States for the Chinese Communists. There was also the recognition that the Chinese Nationalist government was largely corrupt, ineffective and exploitive. The result is that the United States did not intervene significantly in the Chinese civil war and the Communists took over the mainland. We protected the remnant of the Nationalist government when it went to Taiwan, and we still do.

Then China entered the Korean War on behalf of the North Korean Communists and we fought Chinese armies for three years. The American government refused to attack China itself, including Chinese military sanctuaries in Manchuria, thereby insuring that the United States (acting through the United Nations) could not win the war, and it ended in a stalemate.

American Rationales For There Being No Likelihood Of Conflict With China

Over the decades since the end of the Korean War, the American attitude toward China has found reason after reason to be confident that there is little danger of another military conflict with China.

At the end of the Korean War, the American view was that China was impossibly inefficient and inept and could not be a danger to us. There remained hope in the United States that the Chinese Communist government would modernize and liberalize China, making it a good neighbor in Asia. That hope largely evaporated with the Cultural Revolution in China. Not many years later, hope for a liberal future for China was rekindled. The notion was that China was evolving toward democracy. The Tiananmen Square massacre squelched that hope. Then renewed hope was founded on the emergence of the Internet as a source of liberalization in China.

The notion was always that given time, China would evolve in democratic ways, so if we were only patient, time would remove the risk of conflict. As American trade with China has rapidly expanded in recent decades, it has been thought that economic ties have become so close that a rupture is unthinkable. This idea persists. Currently, the most popular notion about China in our country is that China is poorly-led and badly-governed and so will be stuck for years in economic problems and therefore cannot be considered dangerous to the United States.

Meanwhile, China's military capabilities; its geo-political ambitions; and its belligerency keep growing.

What Should The United States Do?

The central questions which arise for the United States about its relations with China are two:

1. What should be America's response to the demands of China for its own special sphere of influence in the Far East?
2. If we oppose China's demands, what is the best way to do so while preserving peace?

The official American position is that we oppose the demands of the Chinese for an area of special influence in the Far East and that we will oppose the methods China takes to achieve its ambition, especially any means that are military. Hence, we are objecting diplomatically to China's building of military bases on artificial islands in the South China Sea, and we are monitoring, and even harassing Chinese military units in the area. We are promising our allies in the region that we will support them in opposing Chinese incursions. We are providing military assistance even to old enemies such as Vietnam, presuming that if the assistance is used, it will be against Chinese aggression.

This current American policy extended into the future will require us to match Chinese military modernization and expansion bit for bit. We would expand the American conventional arms position in the region and provide more and more arms to any nation which will resist China's initiatives.

We are not going farther than this, and this will soon not be enough. China has nuclear warheads. Until now, it lacks long-range missiles that can deliver those warheads to American soil. China is now designing, testing and building such missiles. So is its client state, North Korea. When China and/or North Korea have such missiles, the correlation of power will change dramatically against the United States.

When this occurs, and it is not far away, apparently, then we will likely be unable to stop the Chinese acting as if their desired sphere of influence exists. We are then likely to be drawn into a conventional war in the Far East (naval initially). To avoid such a war, we will have to concede to China its sphere of influence, with all that means of our loss of influence with our current allies in the region.

This would be an unpleasant future. It would be a future in which we first embitter China by our opposition, and then concede to China dominance in the Far East. No more ineffective policy can be imagined.

Because this unpleasant future can be foreseen, some Americans are already planning for a different course in American policy. Some of Senator Clinton's policy advisors say privately that they have written off East Asia into a Chinese sphere of influence and are lobbying the Chinese for continuing access to China's markets — that is, for continuing economic access for the United States in the Far East. They are concerned that a China dominant in the Far East will deny markets to the United States. The logic of their position is that the United States would support, or at least not actively oppose, China's assertion of dominance in the Far East in return for favorable economic treatment by China in the region. This is definitely a possible course of action for the United States.

Already the progressive press is preparing the context of public opinion for such a policy. In an article about the changing state of sea power in Asia which specifically discussed China's challenge to the United States, *The Economist* wrote: "It is understandable that a country of China's size, history and economic clout should want… influence and coercion abroad… Nor is it strange that China should want to prevent a possible adversary (i.e., America) from operating with impunity near its own shores." These are all qualitative, even moral, judgments by *The Economist*. They cloud *The Economist's* objectivity in the very realm of geo-politics which it has chosen to discuss. But from these judgments *The Economist* derives support for China's attempt to substantially lessen the role of the United States in the Far East.

Is there a reasonable alternative over the next decade to conceding the Far East to China? The United States cannot and will not take unilaterally the necessary steps to deny China dominance. The United States can cobble together, perhaps, a group of countries in South East Asia which will attempt to resist Chinese ambitions, but it is likely to be ineffective in the long-run. Already, some of these countries check all important policy decisions of their own in advance with Beijing. These are countries that until a decade ago were strong American allies with no close ties to Beijing. The only significant ally in the Far East for America is Japan. A significant role for Japan in a potential military conflict with China requires that Japan rearm to a substantial degree. This will require very careful moves in domestic Japanese politics and in American diplomacy with respect to Japan.

The other possible ally for the United States in limiting Chinese ambitions is Russia. Already China is involved in adjusting to a rapid increase in Russian power and has even scheduled joint naval exercises for September 2016.

How China Will Respond To A Strengthening Russia

Strategically the Chinese may well be responding to the rapid strengthening of Russian military power in same way that the Japanese did faced with a somewhat similar situation in 1941 — facing a very strong

Russia, Japan turned south toward China and South East Asia and built up its navy. China seems to be doing the same thing now and very possibly for the same reason.

It is important to recall that before World War II the USSR and Japan fought a major land battle on the borders of northern China — much of which Japan then controlled. The Soviets (led by General Zhukov) soundly defeated the Japanese. This caused the Japanese not to join Hitler in his June, 1941 attack on the USSR, which lack of Japanese support may have allowed the USSR to survive. When Stalin was sure the Japanese would not attack the USSR in the Far East (because Richard Sorge, a Soviet spy in Japan, told Stalin that the Japanese would go south instead of attacking the USSR in its east), Stalin transferred the Soviet Far Eastern army (called in the West the Siberian army) of 500,000 men in December, 1941, to Moscow. The attack of the Siberian troops, well-equipped and fresh, was completely unexpected by the Germans. The Soviets inflicted so important a defeat on the Germans before Moscow that the Germans never really recovered from it.

Even without a defeat at the hands of Russian military forces, China is likely to go south for the same reasons the Japanese did — that the United States looks to be an easier nut to crack, and the treasures of South East Asia appear more enticing that getting bogged down in Russia's maritime provinces.

The Russians are likely to know if this is the Chinese decision, and are likely to be happy to see it implemented.

It is going to be difficult, therefore, to get the Russians to join us in containing Chinese ambitions in South East Asia. It might be done, but only via major American concessions to the Russians elsewhere in the world. As we have seen, these concessions might involve acquiescing in Russia strengthening its position in Eastern Europe and in the Middle East.

Barring some such arrangement with Russia, and the rearmament of Japan, the United States will be forced to attempt to contain China unilaterally in South East Asia, and this is going to be very difficult.

South-East Asia: Where China Meets Militant Islam

South-East Asia is one of the two places in the world where China and militant Islam are encountering one another. The other is central Asia. South-East Asia is the more dangerous.

Radical Islam is active in Indonesia, Malaysia and the Philippines. China is moving from the outside on all three, and in Malaysia and Indonesia is active on the inside.

The United States now confronts growing Chinese traditional military and economic challenge to its hegemony in the region, and simultaneously a growing non-traditional political and social challenge from militant Islam.

This, even more than the complex situation in the Middle East, exemplifies the growing difficulties the United States now faces. How should the United States respond?

One way is to get out of the region and let the Chinese and the Islamists fight over the carcasses of the quasi-democratic regimes in the region. These regimes were erected in the aftermath of colonialism. In the brief period (some twenty-five years) of American world dominance (1990–2015), these regimes and their allegiance to us were thought by our countrymen to be the normal order of things. They were not.

For us to retain these regimes as supporters of our version of world order requires us to fend off a challenge from Islam on one side and a challenge from China on the other. And the challenges will increasingly overlap.

It would be easier if one of the challengers were to join us in countering the other. We are not likely to be able to work out cooperation with militant Islam. We may do better with China, but only at the cost of strengthening Chinese influence in the region. And since China is currently a far more potentially dangerous rival than Islam, this may be a course we do not wish to adopt.

In consequence, we are likely to try to repel both challengers, and to fail for lack of will and resources.

Chapter 12

Germany's Geo-Political Ambitions

Underestimating Germany

Americans underestimate Germany just as they underestimate Russia. We consider Russia weak and ineffective, and we consider Germany beaten into a pacifist, progressive quietude. Somehow Washington lulls itself into believing that the Germans do not have coherent neo-imperial ambitions. Just as we are wrong about Russia, we are wrong about Germany.

The German experience in the past twenty-five years is one of the most remarkable in the world, rivaled only by that of the Chinese. Seventy years ago as World War II ended Germany lay in ruins and was divided into four parts, each occupied by a different foreign power (France, Britain, the USSR and the United States). At that time the American Secretary of the Treasury was proposing that all industry be removed from Germany and it left as nothing more than a land of farms. Western Germany was reunified, but until 1989 the German nation was divided into a western and an eastern part, each subject to very different economic and political realities. Germany itself lay on the borderline between Western Europe and the Eastern bloc. Germany was weak and vulnerable. It was a frontier region of a European Union in which France was the dominant influence.

Then the Soviets permitted reunification of Germany under Western governance. In the years since, Germany has come to dominate the European Union, first economically and now politically. The EU can now be considered a German sphere of influence. Germany has seized the opportunity offered by the collapse of the Soviet Union to push the borders of the EU and of the Western military alliance, NATO, east. Now Poland and the Baltic States, the Czech, Slovak and Hungarian states, and all the Balkans are encompassed in the German sphere. Germany now reaches even further east into the Ukraine. Germany's recent geo-political expansion is one of the most remarkable feats in history. It has been accomplished so quietly that most Americans are unaware of it. If they think of it at all, they consider it a peaceful expansion of the European Union — which it is on the surface. But Germany's reunification, recovery and the expansion of its influence is of great significance in world politics.

Russia is the first nation to challenge Germany overtly. Russia did so by intervening in Ukraine when Ukraine tried to join the European Union. In response, the United States moved against Russia in an attempt which had the effect, disguised from the American electorate, of protecting Germany's interests. In support of this policy the United States media demonizes the Russians. These things are done by the American Administration and the American media without careful consideration of what has been occurring in European politics and what it means for the United States.

German Success

The Germans no longer have military ambitions. But they continue to have geo-political ambitions, especially in Eastern Europe. They pursue their ambitions via economic means (the Euro; the single European market, demand for "more Europe", the export of the welfare state) and political means (the EU). They are the world's foremost employers of geopolitical influence (so called "soft-power.")

The Germans invented the modern welfare state in the late nineteenth century under their Chancellor Otto von Bismarck. In consequence, the Germans have had a disproportionate impact on our world and not only through two failed world wars. The Germans seem to have a better grasp of what is needed to manage a modern welfare state. The American welfare state is well on its way to ruining the finances of the United States and with it the ability of the United States to serve as the world's sole superpower.

What the Germans failed to achieve by warfare (1860–1945) they may now be achieving via politics and economics. Politically, the expansion of the EU to the East may gain Germany control of most of Eastern Europe and the Balkans. Economically, the welfare state which Germany has championed may ruin America.

The Fate Of The EU And Why

What should we call the European Union? Is it a nation? Is it a supranational state? Is it a super-state under construction as Margaret Thatcher contended? Whatever it is, its reason for existence may be inadequate. Boris Johnson, who was a leading campaigner for British exit from the EU observed that there was no external threat to hold the EU together.

Apparently Johnson and others did not find the two rationales offered for the existence of the EU convincing.

Those two rationales were geo-political and economic. A key geo-political purpose was to preserve peace in Europe by ending national rivalries which had for centuries led to internecine wars. But when the predecessors of today's EU were created, there was no prospect of wars between European states because the Soviet Union and the United States had turned geo-politics into a two-party game via the Cold War. Even without the EU there was very little likelihood of a European war because Germany was de facto occupied by America and all the main alternative trouble spots were controlled by the USSR.

Economically, the fuller integration of Europe has been a success to a certain degree, but it is not necessary in its current form for those benefits to be realized. For example, the departure of Britain from the EU will not impose substantial economic costs on Britain or the EU. In fact, a key reason for the departure of Britain from the EU was to escape what many believed to be stifling regulation which was causing the stagnation of most economies in the EU. For many of the smaller countries in the EU, of course, there is a substantial economic advantage to being in the EU. But this advantage is offset to some large degree by the existence of the common currency. We will return to this topic later.

Without an external threat and without economic advancement to hold it together, the EU was simply a bureaucratic creation. It was non-democratic because the EU bureaucracy was not directly responsible to the people of the EU. It was a transnational governing body erected over the existing national entities. Since it is unlikely to be democratic under any plausible institutional reform, the EU is grossly bureaucratic and corrupt. This is unfortunate, but it is the way the dynamics of politics work. This is making the EU increasingly intolerable to its members' publics, which is the stage at which we find ourselves.

The collapse of the Soviet Union ended the externally-imposed abolition of war within Europe. Should the EU now collapse as well, we might return to a situation of wars within Europe.

We are left with a situation in which the continued existence of the EU is necessary to prevent overt conflict in Europe, no matter how difficult to perceive that it may currently be. Further, the continued existence of the EU places limitations on the opportunistic outreach of the Russians into Eastern Europe. But, at the same time, the EU facilitates German geo-political ambitions with their potential for involving the United States in conflicts.

The result is uncertain. It will be either a continuing EU which is non-democratic, and peace; or the end of the EU, the return of democracy to the nation states, and likely conflict.

The doctrine that is popular in the United States and which denies this likelihood is one that says democracies do not fight one another. If that is true, then a post-EU, multi-state Europe will survive in peace. But when democracies prepare to fight, they turn themselves into dictatorships of some sort, and so the idea that democracies do not fight is simply an illusion of language. The result will be democracies and war — if only because Russia will interfere with the smaller democracies in a post-EU world and stir up war among them.

Should this be the shape of the future, the history of the EU will acquire a sort of Greek tragedy tone in which the destruction of the EU was inevitable given its characteristics from the very beginning. The EU will be perceived to have not been necessary to preserve peace in Europe, despite what its principle founders may have believed. It was instead a creation which enriched some at the cost of many and was both undemocratic and unnecessary. It may turn out to have been an unfortunate interlude in the history of Europe.

The Difficult Future Of Europe

The Euro plays a major role in the current story of Europe. It played little or no role in the story of the British exit. This is, of course, because Britain had not joined the Euro zone, but had kept its own currency, the pound.

But the Euro is a key driver in the future of Europe. The euro creates winners and losers to such a degree that it cannot be accommodated by normal politics. What is now happening is the split of continental Europe into two conflicting camps — Germany and its satellites in the East and the Balkans, and Southern Europe.

The euro strengthens Germany because it keeps Germany's currency (the euro) at a lesser value relative to the currencies of other countries, so that Germany can export more cheaply to them. If there were no euro, and Germany still had the mark as its currency, most likely the mark would be much more highly valued and Germany's exports lessened considerably.

Conversely, the euro weakens the countries of southern Europe, and France also, because it keeps their currency (the euro) at a higher value relative to the currencies of other countries, so that they are less able to export their products and services. In the case of Greece, the situation is virtually catastrophic. Because Greece is in the euro zone, it cannot sell to foreigners enough to provide employment for its people, nor can it earn enough to service the debt it has from Germany. If Greece had its own currency, it would most likely be much less highly valued than the euro, and Greece could sell much more to foreigners. Employment would be much strengthened in Greece. Whether or not Greece would be able to earn enough to service its debt would depend on the relative value of its currency to that of Germany. But there is little doubt that on balance Greece would be far better off under its own currency than in the euro zone.

So significant is the advantage of the euro to Germany, that it creates a situation in which the government of the EU in economic terms is highly advantageous to Germany. And Germany has effective control of the financial and political situation as well, especially since there is no direct election of the EU's legislative branch (this is the much discussed "democratic deficit" of the EU). Economics, finance and politics determine the impact of any nation or super-nation on its constituent parts. When all three are united in behalf of one section of a nation or super-nation, then that section dominates and benefits, and the other section or sections is (or certainly feels) exploited and misserved.

Americans who know their history recognize this situation immediately. It is the situation of the United States in the several decades before the Civil War. The Northern states dominated the economy, the finances and the legislative branch (the Congress) of government. Using all three, they imposed tariffs for their protection, and used the federal treasury to finance infrastructure improvements for their benefit, which tightened their control of finance and the national economy. In consequence, the southern states felt exploited and misserved. This was one of the major causes of the American Civil War. The north won the war, so the exploitation continued for another hundred years.

We should note the strong parallel between the nineteenth century situation in America and the twenty-first century situation in Europe. During the first half of the nineteenth century, as the American political situation was building toward the climax of the Civil War, the United States was expanding rapidly across the North American continent.

Similarly, today as the euro undermines unity in the EU, the EU is expanding toward the east. Territorial expansion disguised the growing danger within nineteenth century America; it now disguises the growing danger within twenty-first century Europe.

The southern nations of the EU are now in a similar situation to the American south prior to the American civil war. There seems no

resolution for them except escape from the EU, as there was no resolution for the American south except escape from the American federal
union. (Remember that Britain was not an early forerunner of the situation of the European south because Britain was not in the eurozone
and so was not subject to the same iron triangle — finance, economy,
legislature — of exploitation that the European south is subject to.

The question for the future is whether or not the European south
will try to break out of the vise in which it finds itself, or whether it will
continue to suffer economic stagnation and massive unemployment
and political direction from the north. If it tries to break out, will the
Germans be so accepting of other nations' exit from the EU as they
have been of the British exit? If not, what are the likely consequences?
The American consequence was a massive four-year long war. That
seems very unlikely in Europe, but events may lead that way. In any
case, the circumstance will offer much opportunity to the Russian
opportunists and a severe challenge for American policy.

Let us quickly examine the implications of some of the more
important possible combinations and chances that may arise out of
the internal tensions in the EU. If southern Europe (including Greece,
Italy, Portugal, Spain and France) were to exit the euro, then the euro
would essentially become the German mark with other members'
implicit currencies pegged to it. There are pros and cons to a German
mark-euro, but the entire matter is less important economically than
politically.

The most important matters are the implosion of supra-nationality
and German dominated "federalism", and the re-emergence national
sovereignty. Europe after congratulating itself for peace-making in the
world, will be racing back to a nationalist future — that is, to a world
unhappily like its bellicose past.

This will be very unfortunate. Europe in the form of the EU has
been in the strongest position to repel military invasions (except from
Russia) in its history. This is a key reason the Muslim influx to Europe
is peaceful. If this is about to change, it will have potentially great
significance in international politics.

There are, of course, alternative views. For example, one hears from
various pundits things like this: "The United States and Russia are once

more locked in what could be a generation-defining conflict, and Europe is yet again the core battleground."

This makes it sound like Europe is again merely a bystander and possible battleground in a contest over world supremacy like the Cold War between the United States and the USSR. This is wrong. Instead, today the United States is being drawn into conflict with Russia by the EU which is under German influence. Europe is anything but a bystander; anything but passive. This German activism is unfortunate for the United States. The United States has no necessary contest with Russia — instead we have a contest with China in the Far East, and a contest with Iran in the Middle East. This is not the Cold War again, though it has similarities because Western politicians retreat into familiar thought patterns.

Germany is now a mature power; it has emerged from its World War II rebirth. It began in a form of national childhood under the administration of four occupying powers. Germany moved through adolescence as a part of the EU. It is now an adult and is pursuing again its own international objectives in the novel context of the European Union. Peace in Europe is very good. But EU is evolving into a German sphere of influence and Germany is urging the EU eastward — good for Russia's western neighbors domestically, but bad for the peace of the world.

The United States is today backing Germany against Russia. It is a reversal of our position in the first half of the twentieth century when in two world wars we supported Russia (and the Soviet Union) against Germany. America's change in posture is argued to be justified because Germany is now a democracy and integrated into the European Union, one of world's greatest democracies. But as we have seen, the EU itself is profoundly anti-democratic, and German democracy is exhibiting renewed geopolitical ambitions.

As always among the great powers, what appear to be separate compartments of policy in the various parts of the world are actually often intimately related. We have been discussing Europe. But the Middle East is quickly drawn in. The United States is pretending that it is working effectively with Russia against ISIS in Syria. This serves the political purposes of the American Administration in two ways:

1. It suggests that the Administration has an effective response to ISIS; and
2. It obscures Germany's role (and NATO's) in turning a once-friendly Russia into our adversary.

In the past few years the Kremlin has experienced a shift in its perception of Germany's role — and this has important consequences. It means that the world is becoming multipolar not on the other side (Russia, China, Iran) but on our side (the breakup of the United States dominated West into the United States-Britain and the German-led EU). The re-emergence of Germany with geo-political ambitions is potentially (over the next two decades) as important as the re-emergence of Russia and the emergence of China on the global stage.

The split of Europe on economic lines is creating an unstable situation in Europe in which Germany holds many of the cards, and the Russians many also. It is up to Germany to determine if Europe attempts to continue its eastward expansion or instead breaks apart in any of a number of possible ways.

American policy must consider any of the likely results, unless American power is reasserted to such a degree that it prevents the break up.

This is of great importance. The situation is fluid, which means it must be carefully managed in Washington, and neither party is able to do that now. Instead, we are experiencing another example of how the world is breaking apart like humpty-dumpty in the context of an indecisive and ineffective America.

Where Brexit Takes America

The British vote to exit from the European Union seems to have played into Germany's hands.

This does not mean that the British should not have made the choice they made. For the moment, the British choice may have benefited both Britain and Germany.

The British were likely the strongest counterweight remaining in the EU to Germany. This is true in both economic and political terms. With their exit, Germany stands alone in leadership of the European continent.

In addition, there are possible significant gains for Germany in the aftermath of the vote to exit in Britain. For example, if Scotland were to be permitted another plebiscite on leaving the UK, and it were to rejoin the EU, a continental power would have easy access to the North Sea and might even acquire the English naval bases in Scottish waters. This the English have fought successfully for centuries to prevent. Had France controlled Scotland in the time of Louis XIV or of Napoleon, England would probably have been defeated. Had Germany controlled Scotland during the First or Second World War, England would probably have been defeated. Now, if the EU were to gain possession of Scotland, Germany would, as a practical matter, have achieved a stranglehold on England,

From the popular press and the political discussions occurring today, one would think that such considerations no longer matter. People either wish to ignore the possibly of conflict, or have lost the ability to think about it in a well-informed manner. But in the defense ministries of Britain and Germany, these topics are much considered.

The Germans are not obtuse. They are opportunists like Putin — they reached for Eastern Europe and will take what they can hold and do not want the United States getting too excited about the game.

United States weakness is a major contributing factor to the increasing assertiveness of Germany. We are providing a vacuum into which Germany (and Russia, China and Iran) are moving. For the United States to vacate some of its current self-imposed obligations in the world is not necessarily bad, but it should be done in an orderly fashion with a clear conception of what is to follow the American role. Today, an orderly exit is not being made.

Consequences For The United States

In the immediate aftermath of the British vote to leave the EU, world equity markets declined sharply. This was justified by the high level of uncertainty imposed by the potential events we have discussed above. The implications are disconcerting for financial markets, and also for American policy.

In the period of uncertainty now emerging about the EU, the United States will be pulled this way and that by many countries and political groups with differing agendas. In some ways, it will be like our situation in the Middle East where every contestant seeks our support and if it is denied, becomes an adversary.

Chapter 13

What The Politicians
Are Offering As Choices
For America And Our Alternative

We have seen in the preceding chapters that an appropriate policy can be fashioned out of a nationalist perspective. We have seen that it can meet the principles and have the characteristics desired of an effective policy. We can now turn our attention to what our politicians are offering to us as choices for a policy orientation for America.

Before we identify the alternatives in a general manner, it is useful to examine a specific example.

ISIS As A Rattlesnake

Think of ISIS as a rattlesnake.

If a person comes upon the snake, she has three alternatives. The first alternative is to pick up a stick and annoy the snake. That will surely result in the rattlesnake striking at her. With respect to ISIS, this alternative is to attack ISIS without bringing to bear enough force to destroy it. This provokes ISIS to attacks on America and Americans.

The second alternative is to kill the rattlesnake. This requires the person to put on heavy boots and stomp it to death. This approach, when applied to ISIS, the American media has labeled "boots on the ground." It was the strategy proposed by Marco Rubio in the early stages of the Presidential election campaign for 2016, and echoed, perhaps, by Donald Trump.

The third alternative is to walk away from the rattlesnake. In the case of ISIS this means to accept ISIS's proposal that if the United States will stop bombing ISIS, ISIS will not conduct attacks in the United States. The United States might insist that ISIS operatives leave the United States, and for this the United States will effectively get out of the mid-East. This was the strategy implied by Senator Rand Paul in the early stages of the Presidential election campaign of 2016.

How are the three alternatives best assessed?

The first alternative is disastrous. It is the worst by far of the three. It merely provokes ISIS to make attacks on Americans. This has been President Obama's approach to ISIS. It is having the expected result. ISIS is striking at the United States.

The second and third alternatives are sensible choices; one of which ought to be fully embraced by the American government. The second requires a substantial military commitment. The third implies a withdrawal by the United States from an area of the world in which we have been much involved since the end of the Second World War. They are thus very different strategies.

But one or the other should be adopted.

The Opposites In American Policy

The three choices are made obscure by the proclivity of politicians to disguise their real policy by proclaiming not only it but the opposite. Usually both formulations, contradictory though they are, are presented to a gullible media and public. Thus, when America attempts to continue today its previous effort at domination of the world, it is common for an American president to insist that the United States acts only in concert with the expressed intention of other countries. Similarly, when a politician proposes to withdraw from American engagements in much of the world, that politician ordinarily insists that his or her policy will defeat America's rivals and enemies wherever they are found. Thereby being assertive is described as being passive, and withdrawal is described as engagement. Internationalist cosmopolitanism is disguised as something like isolationism and isolationism is disguised as something like cosmopolitanism.

President Obama is clearly an internationalist cosmopolitan. Nonetheless, his procedure has been described as "leading from behind." This description was intended to imply that the United States was only a somewhat passive influence in the world. Yet, in important instance after instance the United States under Obama's leadership has made critical shifts of policy unilaterally (though often it informed allies before decisions were announced). Under Obama's leadership, the United States also directed other countries as to what was expected of them. For example, Russia has been instructed by the United States not to defend its border region against European Union encroachment and China has been instructed by the United States not to attempt to assert its claimed suzerainty in the South China Sea. Obama's is a policy of attempted domination, but one wrapped in a cloak of multilateralism.

An opposite policy would be one of isolationism in the form of the 1920s and 1930s. At that time the United States had far more limited international engagements and obligations than it does today. The United States had fought with the Allies during World War I. But following the war the United States failed to join the League of Nations and committed itself to no significant ongoing alliances. It was free to adopt a policy of isolationism, which it largely did. President Franklin Roosevelt struggled against this policy, but his success was very limited. During the Japanese invasion of China, FDR was able to get the United States to demand Japanese withdrawal and to furnish a tiny amount of aid to the Chinese. After the outbreak of World War II in Europe, the American president was able to get the United States to provide increasing amounts of military assistance to Britain, while still maintaining formal neutrality. In fact, much of the assistance given Britain was, under international standards, an act of war against Germany. At the time, however, Hitler preferred to turn a blind eye to the American acts. Roosevelt altered this posture in December, 1941, when following the

Japanese attack on Pearl Harbor he declared war on the United States. The Japanese assault and Hitler's declaration of war abruptly ended American isolationism.

The United States has seen nothing of isolationism since the end of World War II. There are commentators who have urged such a policy, harking back to Thomas Jefferson's advice in 1801 to the nation to "pursue peace, commerce and honest friendship with all nations, entangling alliances with none." Jefferson's advice has been totally disregarded throughout the last seventy years. Those commentators who have urged respect for his advice have been ignored.

In reality, American politicians have since World War II offered to the American electorate only varying forms of cosmopolitanism. The differences among the forms offered are minimal. This situation was for years described as a bipartisan policy. This was a fair description. Bipartisanship has eroded since, but has not disappeared. Since the controversy over the Second Iraqi War, the differences between the two major political parties over the form of internationalist cosmopolitanism have widened, but the common commitment to cosmopolitanism remains unaltered.

It has seemed at times during the 2016 Presidential campaign that Donald Trump is proposing to abandon the commitment to internationalist cosmopolitanism, but it may be that he is simply proposing that the commitment be updated and modified in its form.

There are many forms that a policy lying between cosmopolitanism and isolationism can take. We have been examining this middle ground.

America As A Hegemonic Power

America's leadership since the Second World War has not been imperialist (colonialist), but it has been hegemonic. That is, America does not seek geographic extension; nor does America seek direct governmental control of other nations. America seeks no expansion of its national territory; and it seeks no colonies. But America has been for decades seeking to direct the foreign and domestic policies of other nations as does a hegemonic power.

It is possible to describe America's policy posture since World War II not as cosmopolitan but as hegemonic. That is, in fact, how it is described in Moscow and Beijing. In this view, it is not merely America's involvement in situations all over the world that is the dominant characteristic of its policy. This is a characteristic shared by many countries which have worldwide interests. What characterizes America is its desire to mold the world politically and economically. In this way, America is an aspirant hegemon. Hegemony is thereby properly perceived as the dominant characteristic of American policy.

Examples of this are available daily. American Congress persons (Representatives and Senators) are continually traveling abroad involving themselves in the affairs of other nations. In many instances America is already deeply involved in those affairs — as for example in Iraq and Afghanistan.

It is possible that what American politicians are offering the American people is not merely cosmopolitanism, but a closet-form of hegemony, which is disguised as cosmopolitanism. That is, attempting to dominate the world is presented as mundane participation in international affairs, like any other nation.

Another mode of rationalization for American cosmopolitanism is a widely expressed and widely supported view that the basic world situation is one of the Western democracies against all others. This view justifies America challenging the ambitions of Russia, China and Islam at once — a position which is likely overreach by the United States. But at least this view has the virtue of recognizing the vacuity of assertions that the world is increasingly made up of democracies — this view recognizes that this is not the case. The fact, of course, is that many of the nations that label themselves democracies today are democracies in name only.

A further rationalization for American cosmopolitanism was given voice by *The Economist* on October 3, 2015. "Imagine a fantasy American administration and Congress set to act in its own enlightened self-interest and to the benefit of the world," wrote *The Economist*. There followed a list of international policy actions recommended for the United States which supposedly were in the self-interest of the United States but which also were to the benefit of the entire world. It is a pillar of such rhetoric that whatever may be imagined to benefit the world is in America's enlightened self-interest and so should be an objective of United States policy. Thus the United States becomes a sort of benevolent hegemon, doing whatever the international community believes to be the world's advantage.

To realists, such a posture seems mere homiletic posturing. It is akin to the observation that if Arabs and Israelis would only work closely together, Palestine could be a much better place. That is true, but to believe that such cooperation is possible in today's world is naïve, however admirable it might seem.

Finally, American politicians seem committed to a form of cosmopolitanism the primary objective of which is the financial gain of themselves and/or their political supporters. This is especially evident in the financial activities of the Clinton Foundation, but the Clintons are not at all the only American politicians who are engaged in various forms of self-dealing. The various rationalizations for American internationalist cosmopolitanism which we have cited above are here revealed to be nothing more than disguises for self-dealing.

Where self-dealing becomes the driving force in policy, there is no longer any rhyme or reason to the result. Policy becomes an undecipherable confusion of actions taken for self-interest and rationalized by whatever policy purposes can be marshalled to disguise reality. Policy is then mush — it has no coherence. The various elements do not correspond to any strategy or even general conception. This has been a major criticism of American policy in recent years — that taken as a whole, American policy makes no sense.

An Imperialist America?

On June 16, 2015, Donald Trump announced his presidential candidacy. In his address on that occasion, he appeared to be suggesting that the United States is the world's superpower and that it should be receiving tribute from other nations, not pandering to them with foreign aid, favorable trade treatment, accepting immigrants who are not qualified for jobs, paying too much for oil, and other things.

Commentators did not seem to get his message. This was true of media outlets on both sides of America's partisan political divide. Perhaps this was the case because Trump's notion that American policy should benefit the American middle class, not merely its establishment, was so far from their ordinary thinking that it was unrecognizable to them. Also, since his suggestions did seem imperialistic, commentators may have rejected them on moral bases.

In a way the obtuseness of the commentators — their unwillingness to hear or consider ideas with which they were not already in sympathy — illustrates the problem Trump was addressing. He was objecting, on behalf of the American middle class, to an American policy orientation — internationalist cosmopolitanism — in which the American middle (working) class is milked for personal gain by the American and international establishment, and in which the American intelligentsia can posture as benefactors of the world. Trump obscured his implicit condemnation of the American establishment by insisting that the beneficiaries of American cosmopolitanism are foreign nations, not private interests.

Regardless of the general un-popularity of Trump's position with the establishment, the position has strong historical roots and is not delusional, no matter how poorly he may put it. If the United States had acted in recent decades more as an imperial power, its middle class would be much better off today — and that is what Trump was saying.

Trump's comments on that day were intriguing because they may have been the first overt (if not eloquent) statement of imperialist ambitions by an American politician since before World War I. Specifically, Trump seemed to seek tribute of various sorts from the rest of the world. In a quick overview, the United States emerged from an anti-imperialist Revolution in which the United States left the British Empire. After World War I, President Wilson helped dismantle the Austrian, German and Turkish empires, and after World War II President Franklin Roosevelt completed the job by helping dismantle the French and British empires. The United States has not acted in an overtly imperial way in the decades which have followed World War II, and all of our mainstream politicians support this cosmopolitan but anti-imperialist mode. The attacks by the left on the United States as "imperialist" are nothing more than propaganda; or they refer not to American actions but to American support for European countries which were formerly imperialist (while ignoring the major role that the United States had in dismantling each of those empires). Therefore, to have Trump declare for the presidency and simultaneously advance an overtly imperial agenda was startling.

The degree of public support for an American imperialist position is unclear.

A look at Roman history reveals a rhythm of decay and revitalization with movement from republican to imperial modes, all this accompanied by massive corruption and insider dealing on a rising and falling scale. In the long sweep of history, one must wonder if the United States is following a somewhat similar path.

American Politicians With Military Backgrounds

America is the world's major and most active military power. It would seem appropriate that American politicians have military experience. However, as a general rule, American politicians have little or no military experience and do not reflect the military culture with its sense of personal and group honor and support. American politicians generally lack experience of both the techniques and the culture of the military. When candidates who run for the presidency do have military experience, they are ordinarily rejected by the electorate, generally at the primary level. This is common in most Western democracies. It has consequences, many of which are unfortunate. There is now in the American Congress a self-conscious grouping of elected legislators who are veterans of our military services. Should they be able to exert a greater influence in the Congress, the country would be well-served.

Part III

The Decay Of Post-World War II Cosmopolitanism

Chapter 14

Lions Led By Donkeys:
The Record Of Today's Cosmopolitans

America continues to have great strengths. It has elite military units which are the best in the world. It exerts leadership in key areas of technology. It has a free and ambitious population. It has some excellent schools and scientific researchers. These are the American lions.

But the American situation today reminds an observer of what the German high command during World War I said of the British army it faced — that the British soldiers were lions who were led by generals who were donkeys. Similarly, America's lions are currently being led by politicians who are donkeys.

In this chapter we discuss how and where the donkeys have led our lions.

Inconsistency, Contradictions, Muddled-Thinking, Pretensions, And Willful Ignorance

Each item in the list above — and we should add a few more: lies, improvising, and expediency — is a political virtue and a policy vice. Each contributes to political success and international failure. America has a surfeit of politicians who are expert at employing these items in the domestic political environment. They do not recognize that when projected onto the international scene, these items become vices which lead to failure after failure.

America gets into wars because of these vices. Compounding the unhappy result, when we persist in these political moves, we fail in warfare.

We are victorious when we set these political moves aside and operate with their opposites — when we plan rather than improvise; when we act with purpose rather than expediently; when we are consistent in our actions; when we are honest about the circumstances we face rather than focus on spinning failure into success; and when we admit reality rather than lie about it to ourselves as well as to others.

Inconsistencies And Contradictions In American Policy
No Urgency With Respect To The War On Terror

On January 22, 2016, CNBC broadcast a lengthy interview with American Secretary of Defense Ash Carter. Carter came across as very professional, engaging, clear, and sincere — in general, professorial. He referred continually to "I…" and almost never mentioned the President.

With regard to the ISIS matter, he gave much detail and discussed strategy, and in the end, there seemed no urgency at all about it. "If we can…," he said; "We are trying to support local forces…," he commented.

He described the conflict as a war, and if so, it must be one of the most leisurely ones in history.

The lack of urgency is understandably disturbing to much of the American electorate.

There seems a subliminal premise in American policy-making that time is on America's side. We do not feel that we have to mobilize for victory. We can address conflicts in a desultory fashion. Carter and President Obama can in this mode assert that ISIS is a paramount threat to America, and then do little about it.

The contradiction between danger and lack of urgency arises because American politicians don't want one "game" — in this case the military response to ISIS — to supersede all the other games in town. That is, a conflict with ISIS can be carried on without disturbing other lucrative aspects of American policy. In a war conducted with urgency, other aspects of our national life are subordinated to victory. This is not happening with respect to the war on terror.

There are many other examples of inconsistencies in American policy. The inconsistencies that are now rampant in American government utterly confuse both our adversaries and allies. Intentioned inconsistencies destroy the effectiveness of policy, but are the essence of successful politics. As a result, politicians make terrible policy makers. It is therefore ironic to see so many American politicians claiming to be policy experts or wonks.

Some inconsistencies are more important than others. For example, the great paradox which lies at the heart of politics in Western democracies is that in practice the individual human being matters very little — there are so many of us — while morally the individual matters most of all. Everyday societies make decisions between the practical and the moral. Any attempt to resolve the choice with finality by giving priority to one or the other results in absurdities and conflict. So our policy is rife with contradictions and what often appear as hypocrisies. Our Congress adopts virtually unanimous resolutions demanding changes in China's dismal human rights record, and then our State Department assures the Chinese leadership that there will be no adverse consequences to China if it pays no attention. This apparent hypocrisy emerges from the clash of the principle of individual human value (human rights) versus the principle of non-interference in the internal affairs of sovereign nations (the Western world order). That this clash of principles arises and is significant is never explained to the American people by administrations intent on posturing as both champions of human rights and of international law.

Yet another example is that our trade policies undercut our economic strength and so are inconsistent with our high level of commitments abroad.

Muddled-Thinking

The continual drumbeat of contradictions invites muddled-thinking (or dumb-think, or confused-think, or wrong-think or multi-think). With muddled-thinking neither intelligent analysis nor right decisions can be made. Examples are many.

- President Obama is a Christian because he says so, even though he was born to a Muslim father and in consequence is a Muslim under Islamic law. But the Islamic state is not Islamic even though it insists it is; nor are the Charlie Hebdo terrorists Muslims even though they insist they are.
- We are at war, but we don't know with whom we are at war. We are engaged against the Islamic state, but we are not at war with militant Islam.
- We are proclaimed to be at war, but soldiers of the other side are considered merely criminals to be arrested and given attorneys and their acts of war treated as crimes. The likelihood of attacks is considered as criminal — will there be "copy-cat" attacks? — instead of being considered as centrally planned and directed acts of warfare — even though coordination may occur among decentralized units.
- Obama: journalists should not attack militant Islam; but freedom of expression will not be limited. To reconcile these two positions, it is only necessary to conclude that the President wishes to be the only one who can limit journalists' expression.
- We are opposed to the terrorists, but our popular media show their acts of terrorism so frequently that the terrorists don't have to release their own propaganda films; the Western media publicize for them.
- We expect all nations to obey international law; some do not; part of international law is that there be no intrusion in the internal affairs of other nations; hence we should not intrude in the affairs of nations that don't respect international law.
- Muslim populations are not implicated by the terrorists in the crimes of the terrorists; but we kill hundreds of thousands of Muslims as collateral damage when we attack terrorists.

- Many political leaders rely on tribalism among voters (they label it "the politics of identity") for their election majorities; but they deny that tribalism exists among those they govern; instead they champion "inclusiveness."
- Future wars are expected to be of short duration and so we don't need extensive military preparedness; but the "war on terror" is asserted to last for decades.
- Many times US politicians (including our President) try to walk one way one day and another way the next, trying to satisfy different points of view in the electorate. This gives American policy the appearance of confusion and contradiction.

These contradictions are so blatant that they cannot be unrecognized by Western political leaders; and the contradictions are more than hypocrisy; it's impossible to believe that intelligent Western political leaders do not intend the contradictions, as Goebbels advised that politicians should.

Pretensions

In several periods in recent years the Chinese have been having trouble managing their currency against massive speculation which drove it down. For any central banker trying to do something constructive with a country's economy, the American supported financial speculation system — we do not do much financial investment — is absolutely maddening. America poses as the champion of a capitalist financial system which invests abroad, but appears in reality to sponsor a vast speculative enterprise. This is another aspect of how the real face of America appears in the world as opposed to our pretensions.

Critics abroad accuse America of many such pretensions:

America as peacekeeper — versus America as always at war;

America as protector of civilians — versus America as killer of civilians on a massive scale in World War II and more recently in Iraq and Afghanistan;

America as champion of women's rights — versus America as creator and distributor of pornography;

America as champion of morality — versus America as champion of license and traditional vices of all sorts;

America as champion of virtue — versus an American popular culture of drugs, sex, and violence;

America as champion of competition and free enterprise — versus America as home of enormous global businesses which form oligopolies;

America the free — versus America the over-regulated;

America the productive — versus America the over-regulated and excessively bureaucratic.

Willfull Ignorance: How America Lost Its Understanding Of Russia Under Bill Clinton's Leadership

In order to give credence to a politically motivated policy, American presidents in recent years have repeatedly removed from our foreign and military service people who were far more expert than they.

A prime example was Bill Clinton's effort to hide American failures in the aftermath of the collapse of the Soviet Union. Clinton was a know-nothing. He had to be tutored on the events of World War II in preparation for commemorative ceremonies for battles that had occurred in the war. Clinton purged the American embassy in Moscow of American Russian language speakers because they were biased against his policies by knowledge of the Soviet Union.

In Clinton's view in the new post-Soviet world, America needed fresh, ignorant, diplomats. The result of our self-imposed ignorance was that we didn't understand what was happening in the transition of Russia to a western-style democracy, and didn't see it veer to the opposite direction when Putin and the security services took over the government. Clinton assumed that the collapse of the USSR would be followed automatically by the advent of a Western-style democracy, and he could not have been more wrong. The following American presidents, Bush and Obama, made the same mistake, so that Putin's Russia emerged suddenly in 2015 as a serious challenger to American power, underestimated and ineptly handled by the American Administration.

The Triumph Of The Round People

The selection for leadership positions of politically-astute people who have no vision and no leadership, who simply play a political game, is now common in American government. These are the round people. The problem-solvers and action-oriented people who prevailed over our enemies in World War II struggled continually against the round people who dominated the bureaucracy that expanded rapidly during the war.

General Vinegar Joe Stilwell, who led American support for China during the war, used to have a reminder to himself, "Don't let the bastards grind you down," except that he expressed it more colorfully in Latin. The bastards he had in mind were the round people, the bureaucrats. There was no difficulty in identifying them. They were, and are, the people to whom the rules are more important than the results. They now dominate American life. This is why America is no longer the "can-do" society of our grandparents. Our politicians are mostly attorneys, and attorneys are the epitome of rules-oriented, results-indifferent, people.

There are many round people in the American policy and military apparatus. There are some results-oriented people. The presence of so many round people explains why our policy experiences so little success.

The US is not leading the world these days, but it is enabling much of it — that is, we are providing the money and other resources in a variety of ways for others to pursue their own objectives — sometimes against our national interests.

The old rule for American presidents was to be sure you are right then go ahead. The modern rule for American presidents is be sure you are right; then seek permission from a coalition who are assembled from foreign dictators, monarchs and politicians who are willing to take American money.

To support internationalist cosmopolitanism and the private agendas it enables, it is necessary for certain people to keep in power. In effect, policy is made to facilitate these purposes. First, it is made to further private agendas. Second, it is made to keep the sponsors of those private agendas in power. The private agendas which drive our policy are not normally visible to outsiders (they are very clear to insiders). But the political purposes which our policy is made to serve can often be perceived by the American electorate, if they look for them.

The making of American policy on the basis of domestic political considerations is very unfortunate. It has the appearance of dimwittedness to much of the American electorate which is impoverished by it. Policy-making for domestic political advantage abandons the reality of the situation abroad. It substitutes pandering to what little the American public knows about a situation and all the misconceptions of the American electorate about the world. It leads to massive inconsistencies because what is said by the American government is whatever needs to be said to put to rest a political issue of the moment. It matters not at all if what is said today is consistent with what was said last week or is consistent with what will be said next week. If challenged about inconsistency, the president or his spokespersons will say that there is no inconsistency and offer many details of each situation to distinguish it from the other, so that different treatments in different contexts can be argued to be consistent with each other. What is needed is not a convincing demonstration of consistency, but merely a cover for the assertion that there is consistency. Then the White House and the media move on to the next topic. A key skill of the president and his spokespersons is the ability to rationalize decisions made on solely political purposes, as if they had an underlying policy logic and were consistent on a policy basis with one another. Posturing of this nature clouds rather than clarifies, but rarely misleads governments abroad.

American Leadership — Inept Negotiators Or Something Else?

Donald Trump accuses American political leadership of being inept negotiators. His condemnation is not quite right. If anything, it is too mild. Our political leadership in recent decades has not been inept at negotiations. They have and do negotiate well for themselves — for money, status, and ego-enhancement. Unfortunately, they abandon the interests of the American people as they negotiate for themselves. This is what the United States gets when individualism and greed are endorsed, while patriotism and self-restraint are despised.

In the chapter below we will turn to each of these items — mirror-imaging, improvising, expediency, inconsistency, and lies — in turn. In the following chapter we will examine spin. But first we will determine what underlies them all.

Policy Diverted To Private Agendas

In recent decades the policy of the United States has been increasingly diverted to serve private agenda. In general, the private agendas are of two types. One is financial — the amassing of wealth for individuals and of profit for businesses. The other is political — the pursuit of ideological objectives of the nation's major political factions and parties.

When our policy is thus diverted from the service of the American people as a whole, it becomes a morass of inconsistent actions as it now is. There is endless discussion and debate about policy and its aspects because there can be no clarity on what it is, hence every commentator formulates his or her own content of discussion. The lack of clarity exists because our policy is not expressible in terms of our national interest. Americans do not know what our policy is because it is nothing more than a mélange of private purposes.

It is instructive to think of the policy process of the United States in Freudian terms. The population, political parties and business entities of the United States constitute a mass of ambitious, ill-coordinated desires and purposes, which, if left to their own devices strive to gratify their desires in complete disregard of the strength of outside forces and which therefore provoke conflict and even risk annihilation. The role of the government's policy apparatus is to represent the outside forces to the mass and so help it survive. That is, the population, business entities and the political parties are rather like the nation's id (impractical instincts), and the policy apparatus of the government is rather like its superego (impractical ethical standards). The government's policy apparatus (the nation's superego) dethrones the self-first principle which exerts undisputed sway over the mass of population, business entities and political parties (the nation's id) and substitutes for it the idealist principle which promises greater success and greater security. The president and his staff are rather like the nation's ego (mediator between two impractical psychological forces: instinct and moralizing). It is crucial that the ego fulfils its role properly to prevent extremism and assure public policy exhibits both wisdom and compassion. When the national ego fails, the nation is endangered. It has been happening in recent decades and the nation is increasingly endangered thereby.

Cosmopolitanism

While America lacks a coherent policy which reflects a national interest, it does have a clear policy orientation which can be identified and assessed. The orientation is what we have termed, for clarity's sake, internationalist cosmopolitanism.

Cosmopolitanism has dominated our policy for seven decades. We now ask: what are its characteristics? What principles underlie it? We are not concerned here with the promises made on its behalf, or the apologies offered for its failures. We are concerned instead with the realities of its performance in recent years. They are very different realities than they were at the outset of our cosmopolitanism in the immediate aftermath of World War II. Cosmopolitanism was then far more successful. This was due to the different circumstances of the time, and that cosmopolitanism had not yet been corrupted into its present form by private interests spouting idealistic objectives.

It is of interest that we must now compare a policy perspective which has years of current results (cosmopolitanism) with one which is untried for almost a century and so can offer only possibilities (nationalism). The fact of a record to be examined might work to the advantage of cosmopolitanism if that record is good. The fact of a record to be examined might work to the disadvantage of cosmopolitanism. From the perspective of the American people, it is a poor record.

In An Age Of Culture War Everything Must Be Politicized

Today America's deepest disputes are not about methods, they are about objectives. We do not quarrel about how to go about reaching agreed-upon objectives. These would be labeled disputes over policy. Today's political conflicts are over the objectives themselves. They are, therefore, about what American culture is to be.

In an age of culture wars, everything must be politicized because there is nothing that is not impacted by culture. In fact, what we mean by culture is the full complement of how a society does things — its attitudes toward all aspects of human life. So if we no longer have a common culture — and it appears that we do not — then every aspect of life is subject to political controversy. It is idle to wish for anything else. There can only be an illusion of cooperation, until the culture wars are ended and a new dominant culture emerges.

In a period of culture wars there are two approaches to leadership. One is to pick a side and try to stamp out the other. This, for example, is what Louis XIII of France did to the French Protestants, the Huguenots. The other is to try to bring the two together by some device or strategy.

It appears that President Obama sought to do the first and has failed. A resilient traditional culture party, the Republicans, continues to dispute much of the left's internationalist cosmopolitan agenda. In part this is because Obama chose to interpret the culture conflict as one in which one side embodied the future and progress and the other was no more than nostalgia or bigotry. So it appeared to him, like Marx earlier, that victory for the one and disappearance for the other were inevitable. He was wrong. What the next president will try to do in the context of a thoroughly politicized conflict of culture is uncertain, of course.

But the culture conflict in America is translated directly into our policy. When the Republicans hold the presidency, America sponsors traditional cultural values abroad; when the Democrats hold the presidency, America sponsors non-traditional cultural values abroad.

Much of the apparent inconsistency and hypocrisy of American policy emerges from this unresolved domestic political conflict.

Politics Without End

In January, 2013, before President Obama had been inaugurated to serve his second term in office, a Republican Senator arrived in Palm Beach, Florida. His purpose was to raise several million dollars to finance his campaign to be chosen president of the United States in the election to be held in November, 2016. He was successful in obtaining the money from donors and was soon campaigning, although unofficially. Unwilling to be left at the starting gate, other Republican candidates began their campaigns, although also unofficially. There was no significant time period between one election and the start of campaigning for the next.

Two years later at a conference in New York City one of the authors of this book was handed a business card by a woman to whom he had just been introduced. The card read as follows (with the last name and state name removed):

Mary L…. MD
  Candidate
2nd US Congressional District State of …

The woman was the candidate of a major political party for a Congressional seat. The election for which she was campaigning was eighteen months away, but Mary was already campaigning full-time. In the past, there was a hiatus after each Congressional election lasting 15 months or so in which politics was set aside and the business of government could be done. Then the election or "silly season" could begin again and no government business was done. This has changed in the past decade as Congresspersons began to spend two or so days each week, year-round raising money for their campaigns. Now for disputed seats (many Congressional seats are certain of the reelection of incumbents), the election process never pauses. America is now a land of unending politics.

The failure of election campaigning in the United States to ever pause has a significant impact on American policy. It means that our policy is continuously conducted for political gain in the context of election campaigning. This is a recent development and one that gives current American policy-making a frenetic appearance.

Given the intense political atmosphere in the United States, is it possible for America to have a coherent policy? Can a politician retain popularity without spinning continually from one posture to another? George W. Bush maintained his war in Iraq and lost his popularity. Barack Obama tried to withdraw from Iraq, and lost his much of his popularity. It is possible to argue that events were driving the decisions of these presidents, but it is more likely that political calculations were driving them. There may be enough time in some president's terms of office for inconsistency to catch up with him or her popularity either because inconsistency becomes itself a fault, or more likely because some unpopular event occurs in part because of inconsistency and it becomes the source of the president's unpopularity.

We turn now to the very important topic of spin, which is the way politicians use the media to communicate with the American people.

Chapter 15

Hitler's Legacy: Modern Political Spin

Spin is now an accepted part of American political culture. As such, it is assumed to be benign. We will see below that the New York Times has even defended it as a positive part of our political culture. It is not. It is fundamentally dishonest and it interferes dramatically with effective governmental functioning. It limits the identification of public problems; it makes their analysis difficult; and it virtually prevents the solution of public problems — of, for example, America's problem with joblessness; of our problem with a slow growth economy; of our decaying infrastructure. Spin denies the existence of problems and so precludes their solution. It is a very bad thing.

Political spin is normally intended to claim credit or deny responsibility for a particular politician or political party for some event. It provides an explanation that benefits a politician or a party. It "spins" the news so that it is advantageous to a politician or a party. It ordinarily does not recognize real problems — it twists them into a benign appearance. It is cosmetic, not realistic. It is ubiquitous in American political culture.

Spin is almost, but not quite, instantaneous in our political culture. For example, to the astonishment and intense displeasure of the governing authorities in continental Europe, Britain and America, the English people voted on June 23, 2016, to leave the European Union. Initially, establishment authorities did not know how to spin the event. But within hours, the establishment-supporting media was working at the challenge. The *Washington Post* published a story online saying that "The British Are Frantically Googling What the EU Is, Hours After Voting to Leave It." People familiar with the prevalence of disinformation in politics realized instantly that the story was most likely a plant. Its purpose was to suggest that that the British electorate had made a mistake in their voting because of their deep ignorance. Twenty-four hours after the announcement of the outcome of the referendum, establishment authorities on both sides of the Atlantic Ocean had developed a full spin and it was pouring from the media as if it were actually news. The vote to exit the EU was due to the ignorance of the British voter. That there may have been an opposing opinion of merit by those who voted for British exit was never considered.

Spin makes it difficult to follow reality. Spin is the continual management of "news" so that responsibility is denied but credit is seized. In the spin environment it is very difficult for public problems to be resolved and for a citizen to become accurately informed.

Spin is propaganda. It is nothing else. It is the modern label for what used to be recognized in the Soviet Union as the "Party Line," and which is still recognized in Communist China in the same way. When one of the authors of this book used to visit the Soviet Union, his Soviet government-assigned companion would cautiously listen to the Voice of America broadcasts each night to get world news, and he would read *Pravda*, a Communist Party newspaper, to get the party line (or the "spin" as we would label it today) the next morning. By this procedure he would know both the reality and the propaganda and be prepared for his day as a Communist Party official escorting an American visitor through the Soviet Union.

The same is done today in America, but not so simply. We pick up news from a variety of sources (mass media, social media, specialized news sources, etc.). Liberals go to *The New York Times* to get the leftist spin and conservatives go to the *Wall Street Journal* to get a rightest spin. The purpose of the spin is to tell us how to interpret the events. A policeman has been shot and killed in an American city, is that a justifiable act of retribution by a discriminated-against African American, or is it a reprehensible murder of a fine public servant by a vicious terrorist?

The *Times* and the *Journal,* according to our political persuasion, will tell us what we should think about it.

Spin In China

Spin begins early in some countries. In China it begins in kindergarten. Children are taught that the Communist Party is all beneficial, and their parents tell them not to be critical — to stay away from politics. One set of exceptions are those people whose parents want them to look to the Party for careers, so that they accept at face value the party's propaganda. The other set of exceptions are those who despite all this propaganda, still think for themselves and are dissidents.

For example, some Chinese report, most people are not very familiar with historical facts, nor do they have the opportunity to gain or keep a balanced perspective through the various campaigns that the party leadership uses to "guide" the reading and characterization of Mao and Communist Party history. "In middle school," a Chinese said, "we read about the stories of the Long March and the hardship they endured in order to expand the party's control and bring well-being to people. This is also the first time that I learn about it at school. The focus of the textbook was rarely Mao himself. In the mandatory history class of high school, we had to study world history and Chinese history. But the textbook for modern Chinese history only had 70–80 pages, filled with many pictures and characters of a relatively big font. We did not have to do any outside reading to get an A for the class. (My high school was one of the best in Shanghai, so it should indicate at least an average level of academics.) Among the textbook 70–80 pages, there should be around 50 pages that address the history of the Chinese Communist Party. Every major historic event, its influence on the history of China and CCP, and the timeline of CCP were briefly given. We were asked to memorize these facts to be prepared for the exam. There was no discussion on Mao's policy or character, except praise of him and a few pictures that portray how the people at the time adored Mao.

"Since we are only expected to memorize the historic facts, most students don't have the time to bother with the real impact of Mao's policy, the implication of the policy, a comparative policy analysis, etc. Apart from the lack of study at school, our parents who experienced the growth barely talk about it at home because they think it is an embarrassing thing to discuss and they don't want us to have interest in politics. They often tell us to keep away from the politics."

Spin In America

Spin is pervasive in American political life. It is so common that it is now generally accepted. People look for the spin they want (as liberals or conservatives) or they just ignore the mass media. For example, when the President holds a conference on race relations, it is intended to show that the Administration is working on this public issue to find a solution. It is given much publicity, particularly on liberal-leaning mass media news outlets. What is not mentioned is that the conference attendees, described as a very much diverse group, were almost all Democrats, that the event was chosen for this particular site because Democrats controlled the governorship of the state, and that a truly inclusive event would have been held in a Republican-controlled state with much less publicity. The event was in fact created for spin and was spun, successfully. America was no better off at the end of the day than before the President's conference. But the Democratic Party was perhaps a bit better off in the mind of the American electorate.

A steady diet of spin is the death any optimal government policy aimed at actually solving major national problems. Political success requires only the semblance of concern and effort, not accomplishment. Spin provides the semblance, and there is no accomplishment. Hence problems fester and worsen for decades and the public becomes increasingly restive.

In the United States, spin is made possible by the incompetence of the news media and its cooperation with the Presidency. About the American news media of today, a White House spin strategist responsible for selling the Obama Administration's Iranian nuclear deal is reported to have said, "All these newspapers used to have foreign bureaus," a former White House media aide has told us. "Now they don't. They call us to explain to them what's happening in Moscow and Cairo. Most of the outlets are reporting on world events from Washington (with government prepared talking points). The average reporter we talk to is 27 years old, and their only reporting experience consists of being around political campaigns…They literally know nothing."

This would not be so bad if the White House were a reliable source of information. It is not. Instead, it has seized the opportunity created by the incompetence of the American news media to spin every story for political effect. The result is that the American public is increasingly fed a diet of disinformation packaged as news.

Our Partisan Media — How It Spins

The American media is full of ersatz news stories. They report no news but instead are little more than professed indignation about certain topics. The topics have been chosen by the media outlet from many options solely on the basis of expected partisan political advantage. The right choses government inefficiency; the left chooses racism.

The major media outlets, print and electronic, are now primarily political propaganda sheets masquerading as news outlets. They run very little news; most articles are fully framed and so are essentially commentary; all have a particular political perspective. Much news that doesn't fit the political orientation of the paper or station is ignored or coverage is minimized. The consequence is that the American public is fed not information but propaganda and elections are simply measures of which body of disinformation has most captured the public attention.

Spin Is Hitler's Legacy

Spin is an advanced form of political propaganda. There has always been political propaganda. But modern Spin has an origin — in Nazi Germany.

We live in a post-Hitler political environment. Hitler has unintentionally dictated the terms of today's democratic political engagement. What we call spin, Hitler still called propaganda, and his propaganda minister, Joseph Goebbels, defined its methods. Nazi propaganda was effective. The modern democratic world has adopted key elements of Hitler's propaganda techniques, though not his purposes. There is not in modern democracies the ethnic hatred and geographic expansionism of the Nazis. There is in modern democracies the propaganda techniques of the Nazis.

These are the key elements of Hitlerite propaganda as developed by Joseph Goebbels:

- A simple lie repeated over and over will eventually be believed.
- The bigger the lie, the more likely it is to be believed.
- Accuse your enemies of what you are doing: if you employ thugs, accuse your opponent of causing violence; if you attack someone, blame the person attacked for inciting the violence.
- Always take both sides of each issue. This confuses your opponents and allows each person to pick which position of yours it prefers.
- When you do one thing, say you are doing its opposite.
- Misrepresent yourself: if you want war, say you are seeking peace.
- Use half-truths: the truth part provides credibility; the non-truth part is the desired deception.
- Use details to create credibility; then provide the lie.
- Take full responsibility for any good event; deny any responsibility for any bad event.

A modern addition to Goebel's list of propaganda techniques is to use technicalities to divert from realities. For example, what difference does it make how many centrifuges the Iranians are permitted under a nuclear non-proliferation treaty if they are not going to adhere to it? Yet supporters of the treaty want to focus on the number of centrifuges permitted. As another example, what difference does the unemployment rate make to monetary policy if the rate no longer measures joblessness? Yet each month there is enormous interest in the announcement of the measured unemployment rate for the past month. This interest is despite the general recognition now that the announced unemployment rate is a very poor measure of undesired joblessness in America.

Technicalities and detail are used as major distractions from the general picture. They are effective with many people, especially where the public attention devoted to the general picture is brief.

The New York Times Endorses Spin

In light of the origin of modern spin and its pernicious effect in modern politics, it is striking to note *The New York Times* defending it.

"There's nothing Orwellian about spin," insisted David Greenberg in *The New York Times*. "It makes politics fun and engages the public."

This is the same as saying, "There is nothing bad about Hitler's propaganda techniques; they make politics fun and engage the public."

Greenberg's comment is an example of political activists in America becoming more and more shameless. Since the Obama White House is never candid — but employing one of Goebbel's techniques the Obama Administration describes itself as completely transparent — activists now endorse dishonesty, labeling it spin. Spin is what the Nazis labeled propaganda and spin adheres to the rules set forth by Joseph Goebbels. There is no way in which it is good for democracy.

Chapter 16

Overestimating Our Strength:
American Decay

Americans Greatly Overestimates America's Strength

"Even with a smaller Army, America's defenses will remain the world's most formidable," the Editorial Board of The New York Times told us mid-way through 2015. This statement does not argue that America's defenses will be adequate to its obligations or interests, only that America's defenses will be greater than any other nation's military. This is of no significance should our rivals combine against us.

The statement implies that America's defense is adequate to its needs, although it does not say so directly. This implication is without meaning unless the writers specify what mission they have for America's defenses. America's defenses are inadequate today for the kind of intervention-oriented policy that the current Administration pursues (all the while insisting that it is doing exactly the opposite). Further military cutbacks will make the inadequacy even greater.

In contrast, America's reduced defenses will be adequate if the United States were to drastically reduce its engagements abroad. Further, with reduced engagements, America will be less of a target for foreign countries, further enhancing the adequacy of our defenses. We will need less defense.

A sane policy connects resources with needs, and therefore is objective about its goals. Today's Administration and its supporters deceive themselves and the country about the goals of American policy and therefore confuse thinking about what level of defense the United States requires.

American National Decay

One of the greatest challenges to a sane policy is to be realistic about American decay and its impact on our capabilities in the world. Too many Americans are in denial about our national decay — some deny it is occurring, others insist it will rapidly turn around in a crisis. Neither is correct.

Viewed as a super-power, the United States is currently in a period of decay. The steady accumulation of wealth in America, even though very unevenly distributed, has softened our nation. Our people have become accustomed to entertainment and diversion. Such a process invites aggression by hungrier and more aggressive people. The United States, with its enormous riches and the wealth of its citizens undiminished by warfare for 150 years, is the world's foremost target. The decay of its government and its society is moving it into the range of exploitation by others.

American businesspeople are forgetting love of country in the exciting profitability of international finance. Our people are busy with entertainment; they are unlearned in the arts of war. Our military has begun to slip into disorder.

Welfare has weakened our poor; luxury has weakened our rich.

The desire to be entertained has replaced for most people any sense of duty to the nation. This is most apparent to our older people who remember the very different attitude of the World War II generation. It is least apparent to the young who have no standard of comparison for the situation in which they find themselves.

American elites no longer send their children into the military.

Bill Clinton was a self-professed draft dodger during the Vietnam War. Since his election and reelection to the presidency, the need for military service on the resume of a presidential hopeful is gone. During the 2016 election none of the most significant GOP candidates were veterans and the same was the case for the Democrats. The signal to American youth that military service is unimportant is far more substantial than the rhetoric of American presidents about the importance of service. Again, acts speak much louder than words.

Today, the large majority of American young men are either ineligible for or refuse military service. In 2014 the American Department of Defense reported that one-third of American young men were ineligible for military service because of physical unfitness (mainly obesity and drug usage); another one-third were ineligible because of inability to pass mental (educational) tests.

The military no longer uses conscription. It is an all-volunteer force. Hence, the American military must recruit from our population to fill the military ranks which are depleted by death, injury, and resignation each year. In 2015 our military was unable to recruit 177,000 people from a cohort of people of the right age numbering at least 21 million.

The Erosion Of American Military Strength

What is happening now is that the core of the American military potential is being eaten out from within.

The United States economy lacks heavy manufacturing breadth for a long war. This has been a consequence of the policies of presidents of both political parties and of the cosmopolitan persuasion in policy. It began under President Ronald Reagan and continued under Bush, Clinton, Bush and Obama.

The vast majority of the young people of the United States are without military eligibility or interest.

Thus the material and human foundation of a strong military is much eroded.

Further, our military has not been honed in large-scale combat now for a decade. It is inevitable that serious weaknesses will exist, including significant weaknesses in leadership.

It is common, and we have cited some above, for commentators to insist that the United States has a much bigger military budget than any of its potential adversaries. In consequence, it is asserted, the

United States is well-defended. But the American military budget, no matter how large, is made up to a substantial degree of elements such as:

1. Disguised social expenditures ;
2. Make-work for politicians' business constituents (weapons we do not need and cannot use);
3. Expensive new technology which has not been tested in combat and will certainly have teething problems when it is;
4. An enormous bureaucracy;
5. Surprisingly luxurious bases and other perquisites for our military officers;
6. Very large pension obligations;
7. Stupendous military travel expenses.

No wonder the United States has difficulty mounting operations abroad without special appropriations from Congress! No wonder the United States declares itself unable to mount more than one expedition abroad at a time.

Additionally, our military budget is heavily weighted with very expensive weapons systems that may now be vulnerable in combat (especially our great aircraft carrier battle groups).

The Republican Congress in an attempt to control federal spending has imposed sequester on the budget of the Defense Department. The rigidity of sequester (essentially, it is a percentage cut in every line item appropriation), has prevented a priority-driven allocation of funds by the Defense Department. The American military cannot now be managed intelligently. This is something that it is very important that a new president should rectify.

Finally, the Obama Administration's implementation of a cosmopolitan policy has involved demoralization of the elite units of our military.

All this combines to create a concern that the United States is not buying at all the amount of effective defense that the size of its military expenditures suggest.

America's Situation Is Now The Opposite Of What It Was Before The Second World War

Before the Second World War, the United States had great political and moral strength internally, but was militarily unprepared.

Today the United States is much more militarily prepared than in 1941 but has significant political and moral weakness internally.

By coincidence, design, or even collusion, America's rivals are steadily stretching American capability so that it cannot cover all the United States' commitments. These commitments have been made explicitly by alliance or implicitly by promise. The result of contracting American capability is that vacuums of power are being created in assorted spots in the world. The vacuums invite our rivals to increase their own reach. As this occurs, the United States falls further behind in meeting its commitments. This is the dynamic of American regression.

The United States Can Win Battles But Not A War

"Americans undoubtedly have the most powerful military on earth and are often prepared to fight. But even though they win all the battles, they seem incapable of winning a war, as in Vietnam or Iraq," a Russian commentator is reported to have said. This conclusion seems to leap out of recent history and is widely accepted abroad — not just in Russia.

This judgment brings to mind France in 1940. In 1940, France was held by most to be the world's strongest military power. It had a large and well-armed military force and had defeated Germany only 22 years earlier in World War I. But it was hollow inside. Its generals and its strategic and tactical thinking were all outdated, and it had no strength of will in its government. So when Germany attacked in the spring of 1940, France collapsed after a few weeks. The concern is that America today is very similar — a military strong on the surface and widely thought to be the world's strongest power, but poorly led by both military and civilians and without strength of will in government. If this analogy is accurate, then the oceans protect us from a Chinese invasion, but we are going to lose some big pieces of turf in our spheres of influence.

From Decay To Disaster

Decay to disaster is a pattern that has been repeated many times in history in all regions of the world. It now endangers America.

An instructive example is the fall of the Eastern Roman Empire in the mid-fifteenth century to the Turks. The Roman capital, Constantinople, was the largest and best fortified city in the world. It had evaded capture for some four hundred years. Complacency and wealth allowed people to get self-indulgent and weak. When a strong enemy appeared, some twenty-five thousand men of fighting age were in the city. Only five thousand were willing to fight on the walls to defend the city. Ten thousand would have been sufficient to defend the city successfully. But those who would fight were too few to hold the city. When the city was captured, all the men had refused to fight were either killed or enslaved. It wasn't that they had no reason to fight, they lacked the courage.

Some people believe that with a major challenge abroad there will be a resurgence of patriotism, duty and sacrifice in America. This is possible, but not at all certain, and it is likely to require a large overt act on behalf of our adversaries, rather like the Japanese attack on Pearl Harbor in December, 1941. Absent such an attack which unifies and energizes Americans, this nation may no longer be able to project power abroad on a scale required by its commitments.

Abnormal Immigration In America

Invasions can occur peacefully by abnormal immigration or violently by military forces. The United States is well-protected by its oceans from violent invasion; it is not protected from peaceful immigration. There are two types of immigration. The United States has long experience with one. It is now experiencing the second. Normal immigration welcomes immigrants who are assimilated into a nation. Abnormal immigration involves immigrants who are not assimilated but instead become a militant sub-culture within a society which ultimately attempts to displace the dominant culture.

Peaceful abnormal immigration has a long history of preceding violent invasion. This was the process that destroyed the Roman Empire.

First, barbarian tribes appeared on the borders of the empire begging for refuge from other barbarians who were their enemies. Often, the Romans permitted them to enter Roman territory. Thereafter, the new residents of the Empire rose against it violently, or joined outside barbarian invaders against the Empire. Ultimately, after a few centuries, the Empire collapsed in the West and was replaced by barbarian kingdoms. The process was one of slow, peaceful infiltration followed by violent uprisings. This process may be underway in Europe and America today.

The Rule Of Democratic Failure

There has emerged, in the past century, a rule of the failure of democratic government. It involves a process in which democracies identify problems and then fail to address them. Democracies virtually always fail to address major problems because there will be a political faction (a party, or the left or right generally) who will insist that the problem is not real or can be resolved without stress. That position will always carry the way with a majority of voters who cannot tell where the truth lies and so will always choose the less costly alternative.

Modern democracy emerged after World War I — not in formal structure but in actual practice. We saw this dynamic first in the run-up to World War II in Europe. We have seen it since many times: in Europe, in the United States, in Southeast Asia, and in Japan.

Authoritarian regimes count on such a process in democracies and act accordingly. Because of the inability of democracies to confront problems in a timely fashion, all the day-to-day "news" of the democratic regimes is simply noise. The result is clearly predictable, no matter what the unique path which is wandered to arrive there. It is always the same: an ability to anticipate and a failure to act, which ends in crisis.

A powerful recent example involves Greece. In September 1996, the finance minister of that country wrote to Greece's prime minister that they could lead the country via reforms in a truly European direction. In the years since, a handful of politicians have tried to get Greece to cut back its borrowings to avoid the current debt crisis. All failed.

"Their reform proposals were fought by their colleagues in parliament and savaged by the media and labor unions," a reporter tells us. They invariably found themselves sidelined. America is now strongly exhibiting the characteristics of democratic failure. There are multiple warnings about the decay of American strength. There are multiple warnings about the financial morass into which the American government is sinking, including its negative impact on our military strength. There are multiple warnings that we are failing to address the increasingly blatant challenges offered by radical Islam, Russia and China. There are some few politicians who seriously propose that we address some or all of these problems. But there is a vocal and persuasive body of political opinion that denies the reality of each of these challenges, and insists there is no need for serious action. The result is that year after year each of these problems worsens. At some point in the future, it will seem that for American to follow the pattern of democratic failure was, at this point, a death wish.

A sane policy would identify and seek to resolve each of these major challenges.

Chapter 17

More Sleepless Nights: Ineffective Policy

In our world, in which spin dominates political communication, the president generally is able to claim that he is already doing everything that is advocated by critics. This is because White House spin includes claiming that the president is on both sides of all issues.

In reality, the sane policy examined in this book is very different from what is now being practiced by the American government. To see this, it is necessary to get beyond White House spin. A policy should be judged by its results, not by its intentions or the rhetoric which surrounds it. Whatever his intentions, the results of President Obama's policy are violent chaos in and around the Muslim world and the increasing hostility of our Russian and Chinese rivals. Thus, the evidence is that the policy is misguided and inept.

Obama's perspective seems to be that the Islamic world is a helpless victim of Western imperialists. Hence, America should provide assistance to Muslims. The terrorists are flies in the ointment and so are not Muslim at all.

President Obama has a geo-strategy: subordination of the US to international organizations, "partnerships" and norms. Trump's geo-strategy is very different: American strategic independence.

Obama has no preparation for crafting a strategy and he confuses tactics with strategy. Sound policy begins with a clear strategic concept, as is offered in this book. For example, speaking for the President,

American Secretary of State, John Kerry described America's plan for countering violent extremism in these terms: "Show the world the power of peaceful communities, and tackle bad governance that breeds frustration." As a tactical expression, this is understandable. It represents the American government posturing before the world. As a strategic plan, it is nonsense because it cannot be implemented in a time frame or upon a scale adequate to undermine radical Islamism.

Obama lacks any strategy, but he does have a coherent orientation — he seeks an accommodation with militant Islam. This gives his decisions a certain consistency. But viewed from the perspective of democratic nationalism, his actions seem confused and incoherent. This is why it is legitimate to criticize Obama both for being consistent and inconsistent. Which it is depends upon the perspective from which the judgment is being made.

A Man Of Talk

Obama is an attorney, professor and community organizer; he is not a man of national action. He is a man of internationalist cosmopolitan talk. When he is matched against a man of pragmatic action — like Vladimir Putin — the difference in results is clear. The professorial and agitator approach is to say everything, do nothing of significance, shuffle, double-talk and change the subject. A German maxim of conflict is as follows: No stinting, but stunning! That is, don't hesitate in the presence of the enemy but knock him out. Obama stints always and never knocks an enemy out.

The result, in one significant example, is that of Syria. The American Administration created a civil war by insisting that the Syrian dictator had to go, and then permitting him to stay. The Russians then moved into the vacuum created by the Americans and propped up the dictator's regime, gaining a foothold in the Middle East in the process. This was an important policy failure of the Americans because it involves Russia.

Obama is not a progressive as his supporters insist, and he is not an incompetent as his opponents insist. He is an internationalist cosmopolitan revisionist — an agent for a different concept of America and its interests. His view is of the world as revolutionaries of the Third World perceive it. He views America until his presidency as racist, exploitive and imperialist. He has been trying to mitigate or reverse this record. Seen in this light, his policy becomes intelligible. But because Obama lacks confidence that the American people will support his revisionism, he pursues his concept without acknowledging it publicly.

The Obama Administration is often criticized for not having a complete strategy. This may be true in an academic sense. But the Administration does have a perspective and goals — key elements of a strategic framework. Its perspective is that of a third world anti-colonialist. Its goals are to limit the damage America does in the world — as it views the world. It has been trying for seven years to reorient American policy so that our adversaries in China, Russia, and the Islamic world are no longer hostile and so that nations which have been suspicious of us in Africa and Asia are no longer suspicious because they themselves have been transmuted into international cosmopolitans. Because the Administration has a different perspective and goals than those which have driven American policy for decades, many people cannot recognize them and over-impute to the Administration confusion, not design. In effect, from the traditional perspective of American policy, this Administration is on the other side. What the Administration does intentionally, its domestic opponents too often misread as unintentional incompetence. The understanding of the Administration which explains its actions completely is that the Administration is on the side of our third world critics. The rhetorical aspirations of third world nations are what America should become.

The tragedy of the current situation is that President Obama has set the stage for another great war all the while apparently believing that he was doing the opposite. In this he is like one of his heroes, Woodrow Wilson, who tried to reorganize the world in the interest of peace and instead set the stage for World War II. Wilson did so by imposing an idealistic view of the world on its reality; Obama has done the same.

This description comes closest to illuminating President Obama's numerous contradictions. He is not a consistent ideologue, whether social democrat, Islamist, Marxist, or anti-colonial liberationist. Nor is he an integrated and harmonious blend of any or all the options. If an academic term is sought, it might be that the president is a "conflicted assimilationist." He seeks to assimilate all peoples into an anti-colonialist cosmopolitan whole, but he is very conflicted about the means to do so.

Obama's perspective on international politics seems to be that action-oriented geo-politics is now outdated and practicing it, as Putin does, is self-defeating. So Russia's grabbing of Crimea is pointless and destructive to Russia's interests, as is Russia's military intervention in Syria and support of Assad. His broader notion seems to be that the important things done in international politics are done by diplomacy, and forceful action, such as Putin undertakes, undermines his ability to accomplish things in this sphere.

The position of the Obama Administration is that America doesn't engage in international power politics (realpolitik). Instead, America promotes the global rule of law. From a realist perspective, this position is pure hypocrisy. It is therefore fashionable among elite circles. The fact — realism — is that Putin is sitting on the Crimea and will never give it back. In addition, Russia is stronger geo-politically and militarily for possessing the Crimea.

The Obama Administration sometimes stresses strategic patience to camouflage its indecision and inaction. The term, "leading from behind," is sometimes used to camouflage its inability to provide direction to the world. Sane policy is characterized by decision and action; it is able to give direction to the world.

A Key Principle Of Modern Politics — Persistence Reveals Intent

When smart people persist in a course of action the results often reveal their intent. This is a key principle of modern politics. It is necessary to have such a principle because spin means that politicians will be intentionally misrepresenting their purposes. They will be saying that they want to do THIS, but they will be doing THAT over and over. They are smart — all successful politicians have that form of intelligence which is manipulative of others — and know what they are doing, however they misrepresent it.

So, when politicians persist in a course of action over long periods of time that has certain clearly observable consequences, they should be presumed to intend those consequences, whatever else they say — however much they deny it. Thus, American politicians who have persisted for decades in policies that undermine the family should be presumed to intend that result (as they do in Sweden but there admit it). In the United States, some people criticize politicians for what they presume are unintended consequences of government policies that result in destruction of the family, and presume that the consequences are not desired. The politicians deny any intention to destroy the family. In fact, the politicians intend that consequence. It creates generations of people who support those politicians.

Similarly, Obama has acted to undermine American power in the Islamic world. His critics presume he does not intend this. But he has persisted for years in the undermining of American power; he cannot miss the consequences of his actions in undermining American power and so he should be presumed to intend to undermine American traditional spheres of influence — whatever denials he may make.

President Obama's Comments On Key Issues Of American Policy

On September 28, 2015, President Barack Obama spoke to the United Nations General Assembly (his speech is available on the White House press website). The speech was his final one to the UN General Assembly as president of the United States. It was a summary of his convictions about the world and American policy. Below, key comments from the President's speech are quoted and responses offered from the perspective of sane policy. Sometimes sane policy agrees with President Obama; sometimes it does not agree.

On Global Power Politics

"Effectively, [my political opponents] argue for a return to the rules that applied for most of human history and that pre-date this institution: the belief that power is a zero-sum game; that might makes right; that strong states must impose their will on weaker ones; that the rights of individuals don't matter; and that in a time of rapid change, order must be imposed by force."

(President Barack Obama's speech to the United Nations General Assembly, September 28, 2015.)

A person might answer from the perspective of sane policy:

- Power politics has applied for most of human history and still does;
- Power is not a zero-sum game;
- Might does not make right;
- Strong states do not have to impose their will on weaker ones — this is exactly what sane policy wants the United States to stop doing in trying to impose the Western world order on the world;
- Rights of individuals do matter;
- Order does not need to be imposed by force — sane policy wants the United States to stop trying to impose order by force in areas such as the Middle East and Eastern Europe.

On The Record Of Cosmopolitan Policy

"Over seven decades, terrible conflicts have claimed untold victims. But we have pressed forward, slowly, steadily, to make a system of international rules and norms that are better and stronger and more consistent…It is this international order that has underwritten unparalleled advances in human liberty and prosperity. It is this collective endeavor that's brought about diplomatic cooperation between the world's major powers, and buttressed a global economy that has lifted more than a billion people from poverty. It is these international principles that helped constrain bigger countries from imposing our will on smaller ones, and advanced the emergence of democracy and development and individual liberty on every continent…" (President Barack Obama's speech to the United Nations General Assembly, September 28, 2015.)

A person might answer from the perspective of sane policy that these are indeed accomplishments of the past seven decades. But the recent perversion of these efforts into a system of elite self-enrichment is ignored by the President.

Obama's Characterization Of His Opponents

"Even as our economy is growing and our troops have largely returned from Iraq and Afghanistan, we see in our debates about America's role in the world a notion of strength that is defined by opposition to old enemies, perceived adversaries, a rising China, or a resurgent Russia; a revolutionary Iran, or an Islam that is incompatible with peace. We see an argument made that the only strength that matters for the United States is bellicose words and shows of military force; that cooperation and diplomacy will not work…"(President Barack Obama's speech to the United Nations General Assembly, September 28, 2015.)

In effect, Obama identifies realism with force; his speech is directed against militarism, which he says confronts him in America, although it does not confront him anywhere at this point. He is against Hitler and Mussolini and Tojo — none of which confront him; but he does not say or admit this. He is leading a crusade against Fascism, seventy years after it disappeared. He pretends it exists because it gives him an easy opponent to denounce.

The Status Of Dictatorships

"The history of the last two decades proves that in today's world, dictatorships are unstable." (President Barack Obama's speech to the United Nations General Assembly, September 28, 2015.)

A person might reply from the perspective of sane policy that the position of Syria's dictator hardly seems unstable. President Obama has been trying to drive him out for years. Further, Saddam Hussein could only be toppled by American military force. The clerical dictators of Iran have not been dislodged by American efforts. In fact, very few modern dictators have been overthrown. So if dictatorships are unstable, they are not particularly vulnerable.

Intervention Abroad

"Consider Russia's annexation of Crimea and further aggression in eastern Ukraine. America has few economic interests in Ukraine. We recognize the deep and complex history between Russia and Ukraine. But we cannot stand by when the sovereignty and territorial integrity of a nation is flagrantly violated. If that happens without consequence in Ukraine, it could happen to any nation gathered here today." (President Barack Obama's speech to the United Nations General Assembly, September 28, 2015.)

A person might respond from the perspective of sane policy that America can and often does stand aside when the sovereignty and territorial integrity of a nation is violated. The danger is that Obama's position requires America to intervene in situations all over the world. It is an expression of policy that makes America the policeperson of the world The only defense of his position that Obama offers is a homily — if all aren't safe, none are safe — that is demonstrably false. In fact, many people in the world are safe when yet others are not. This is the case in the world as a whole, and it is true in the United States itself.

Principles Of President Obama's Policy

Above, we have responded in detail from the perspective of sane policy to key comments made by President Barack Obama in his concluding speech to the General Assembly of the United Nations.

Obama's speech at the UN can also be read as a response to his critics who charge that he caused the debacle in Syria and the rise of ISIS. In his speech, Obama does not answer the charges directly, but does so indirectly by listing a series of general principles he insists apply in Syria and Ukraine. The principles are:

- Military force alone cannot suffice to resolve a conflict
- There must be a political settlement
- Dictators fall so it is futile to back any

- Involved nations must act together to bring about a solution to conflict
- Diplomacy is the ultimate solution to a conflict
- Any other view is outdated in this century

These are the basic tenets of President Obama's policy as offered to the public.

There is nothing wrong with each of his principles, but offered as a universal substitute for force they are futile. It is force that is behind the conflict in Syria, and force is necessary to end it. Force is not the problem; it is part of the solution. Only in unusual situations can force be ended by diplomacy alone. This is a realistic appraisal.

Rejection of force in almost every circumstance is not only President Obama's position — it is the position of most European politicians. The proposal is to rely on diplomacy to address conflict everywhere. Ironically, it is made possible only by American military protection of Europe. Diplomacy is ordinarily unsuccessful as in Syria, but the European politicians do not care. Meanwhile, they profit from the efforts to make peace and from commercial exchanges with the adversaries. Obama seems to be trying to put the United States into the European position.

The Americans and the Europeans often have a diplomatic entrance to an arena of conflict, but they usually lack a realistic endgame. They negotiate among themselves and insider fantasies call the tune. The tune changes with domestic political winds. Last week the slogan regarding ISIS was victory or death. This week, victory is postpone-able because of the migrant influx into the EU has become a political hot potato. Next week, with another terrorist attack in Europe, the slogan is again death to ISIS. It is a feckless policy.

When America joins the Europeans in this approach, the world is left without a stabilizing superpower.

Chapter 18

The Next Step: A New Politics

What is the next step in the complex struggle over the direction of American policy? It is a new form of domestic politics in the Western democracies. The new form is likely to dominate Western politics for the next decade. But it is a hidden form of politics — it is intentionally disguised. It is the creation of the political establishment. It involves a deeper exploitation of Goebbels' theme of propaganda. Many people will not even realize it is happening. But it will hold the key to our futures.

The Establishment Rallies

The new politics is beginning now in Britain. The English people have voted to leave the European Union — they voted for Brexit — the British exit. This is a vote for a clear change, but the government is controlled by politicians who have supported remaining in the European Union. Both major British political parties opposed the British exit and campaigned against it. Parliament is dominated by members who opposed exit.

Yet, the British majority voted to leave the EU. The people in power in Britain did not call a Parliamentary election in the aftermath of the Brexit vote. Instead, the leader of the Conservative Party which has the majority in the House of Commons, and who led the campaign to stay in the European Union, resigned. He was not replaced by a supporter of Brexit, but by another Conservative leader. She vowed to implement the British exit. She proposed a lengthy period of negotiations with the European Union over the terms of the British exit. She appointed supporters of Brexit to her cabinet.

On its face, this is fine. It is intended to reassure the majority of the British electorate who voted for Brexit that the government will faithfully implement their intentions.

But something very different is underway. It is explicit if those involved know now what the process is likely to be. It is implicit if those involved do not yet comprehend what they will themselves do in the future. It is possible, of course, for people to not know what they will do in the future, although it is already written, so to speak, in the cards. That is, given their objectives, they will make decisions that others can already see, even if they do not yet see themselves making those decisions.

What is beginning in Britain is a process in which leading politicians will posture as willing to make the changes supported by the electorate (exiting the EU) but behind the scenes are preparing to reverse the verdict of the people. Officials are being placed in charge of the exit who do not support it. Those politicians who do support the exit are being placed in offices which do not directly bear on the exit negotiations. The process is going to be lengthy, allowing opponents of the exit time to mobilize opposition to exit. All this will be done under a posture of support for the people's will — that is, for exit.

This is a subtle, disguised game which most people will not realize is being played. The game uses time and deception to thwart the popular will. Those who are acting in this way to deny the public purpose will justify their actions by representing the popular opinion as uninformed, prejudiced, ignorant and misguided. They will denounce it as "populist." They will seek to build support for a reversal of the vote to exit the EU. The reversal may be in whole or in part. If whole, Brexit will be reversed. If part, the exit will be partial. What occurs depends on how successful the opponents of Brexit are in trying to avoid it.

This is a new political dynamic that will dominate the next few years in the West. It is going to happen in the United States also, if the United States moves in the anti-internationalist cosmopolitan direction now embodied by Donald Trump.

In America (and in other Western democracies) there has been building public opposition to many aspects of government policy. There is dissatisfaction with both economic circumstances and anti-terrorist efforts. There is a shift in public support toward parties and politicians that promise significant change. The politicians who control the parties which have been in power — the political establishment — are seeking ways to thwart these purposes of the public. The process is likely to be the one we have just described in the context of its emergence in Britain.

This new political dynamic is being initiated by the establishment in defense of its insider-based advantages. It is an expression of expediency. It involves no ethics, simply a will to power. It is our immediate future.

As a result, the American people may have to wait a little longer for the replacement of a policy which is insane from their perspective, by one which is sane in that it benefits them.

Bibliography

Ahmed Rashid, *Descent into Chaos*, New York: Penguin, 2008, pg. xxxviii.

Adrian Croft, "NATO Defense Spending to Fall This Year Despite Russia Tensions", Reuters, https://www.yahoo.com/news/nato-defense-spending-fall-despite-russia-tensions-190453734--business.html?ref=gs, June 22, 2016.

Ben Rhodes, quoted in *The New York Times*.

Colin Mason, *A Short History of Asia*, London: MacMillan, 2000, pg. 53.

Dalibor Rohac, "Who will Stand up for Cosmopolitanism?" http://www.aei.org/publication/who-will-stand-up-for-cosmopolitanism/American Enterprise, July 11, 2016.

David Greenberg, "Why Spin is Good for Democracy", *The New York Times*, http://www.nytimes.com/2016/01/15/opinion/why-spin-is-good-for-democracy.html?_r=1, January 14, 2016.

Gaidar Institute for Economic Policy: "Russian Economy in 2014 Trends and Outlooks (Issue 36)", http://iep.ru/files/text/trends/2014-eng/Book.pdf, July 30, 2016.

Ghassan Michel Rubelz, "To Tame Terror, Integrate Muslims into the West," *The Palm Beach Post*, January 29, 2015.

John Kerry, "Trump's Plan for Countering Violent Extremism", *The Wall Street Journal*, http://www.wsj.com/articles/john-kerry-our-plan-for-countering-violent-extremism-1424305659, February 19, 2015.

Michael R. Gordon, "Survey Points to Challenges NATO Faces Over Russia", *The New York Times*, http://www.nytimes.com/2015/06/10/world/europe/survey-points-to-challenges-nato-faces-over-russia.html, June 10, 2015.

Major General F. W. von Mellenthin, *Panzer Battles*, New York: Ballantine, 1956.

Matina Stevis, *The Wall Street Journal*, July 11, 2015.

Plutarch, *The Lives of the Noble Grecians and Romans*, Chicago: Encyclopaedia Britannica, Inc., 1952, pg. 562.

Polina Tikhonova, "China Defends Military Expansion in South China Sea", Politics, http://www.valuewalk.com/2015/11/china-defends-military-expansion-south-china-sea/, November 27, 2015.

President Barack Obama's Speech to the United Nations General Assembly, September 28, 2015.

Richard A. Bitzinger, "Southeast Asian Naval Expansion and Defense Spending," IMDEX ASIA.

Robert D. Kaplan, "Countering Putin's Grand Strategy," *The Wall Street Journal*, http://www.wsj.com/articles/robert-d-kaplan-countering-putins-grand-strategy-1423700448 , February 12, 2015.

"Rockefeller," *The Islander*, June 11, 2015, Section 5, pg. 6.

Scott Gilmore, "Putin's Russia is a Poor, Drunk Soccer Hooligan", *The Boston Globe*, https://www.bostonglobe.com/opinion/2016/06/21/putin-russia-poor-drunk-soccer-hooligan/0HjzEzAUT4J58guK170F0H/story.html, June 22, 2016.

Sigmund Freud, *New Introductory Lectures on Psycho-Analysis*, New York: W.W. Norton & Company, Inc. 1932.

Steven Rosefielde, Kremlin Strikes Back: *Russia and the West after Crimea's Annexation*, Cambridge: Cambridge University Press, forthcoming.

The Editorial Board , "North Korea's Nuclear Expansion," *The New York Times*, http://www.nytimes.com/2015/02/27/opinion/north-koreas-nuclear-expansion.html, February 27, 2015.

"Who Rules the Waves?" *The Economist*, October 17, 2015, pg. 65.

The Editorial Board, "Military Cutbacks Make Sense", *The New York Times*, http://www.nytimes.com/2015/07/25/opinion/military-cutbacks-make-sense.html, July 25, 2015.

William Schomberg and Kylie Maclellan, "UPDATE 1-Brexit leader Johnson says EU on same doomed path as Hitler", Reuters, http://in.reuters.com/article/britain-eu-johnson-idINL5N18C06X, May 15, 2016.

Zachary Keck, "5 U.S. Weapons of War Russia Should Fear", *The National Interest*, http://nationalinterest.org/feature/5-us-weapons-war-russia-should-fear-12026, January 14, 2015.

Index